How to Restore & Repair

Furniture

step-by-step guide

How to Restore & Repair
Furniture
A step-by-step guide

Consultant Editor:
Alan Smith
Revised and updated by Chris Jarrey

SILVERDALE BOOKS

A QUANTUM BOOK

This edition published by Silverdale Books,
an imprint of Bookmart Ltd., in 2005

Bookmart Ltd.
Blaby Road
Wigston
Leicester
LE18 4SE

Copyright © MCMXCIX
Quantum Publishing Ltd.

This edition printed 2005

ISBN 1-84509-110-8

QUMSGRF

Printed in Singapore by
Star Standard Industries (Pte) Ltd.

CONTENTS

How to use this book

As everybody knows, hiring a professional to restore a piece of damaged furniture to its former glory is expensive – and with a little time and patience you can achieve a very similar result with your own endeavours. This book is designed for enthusiasts who not only want to save money by restoring their own furniture but also seek the satisfaction of knowing they have done it themselves. It is a comprehensive manual directed both at the novice and at the more experienced restorer; it tackles every aspect of furniture restoration from simple cleaning methods to intricate cabinet repairs. This book will equip you with the basic knowledge for comprehensive restoration projects, however, if you are in any doubt I recommend that you consult an expert; inexperienced restoration can greatly devalue antique furniture.

For convenience, the book is divided into three sections: 'Woodwork', 'Other materials', and 'Upholstery'. Each section has a few pages detailing the essential tools and materials relevant to that section, followed by a series of how-to-do-it projects. All the projects are illustrated by detailed photographs and easy-to-follow drawings, which show you exactly what to do.

WOODWORK

This section shows you how to deal with everything from wobbly chair legs to blistered marquetry, how to clean furniture without ruining it, and how to achieve a professional lustre when polishing. If you develop a 'feeling' for restoring wooden furniture, you will need specialised tools and ultimately a work space in which to use them. Advice on how to set up a workshop is therefore included in this section.

OTHER MATERIALS

This section shows you how to restore all sorts of defects in furniture that is not derived entirely from a tree trunk. Everything from plastic to *papier mâché* and glass is covered. All you need to know about restoring cane and rush furniture - which is both vulnerable and frail – is also contained in this section.

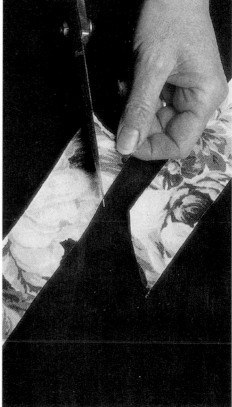

UPHOLSTERY

Upholstery is a world unto its own. There are many ways to make a cushion and many ways to render a soft chair. This section makes it simple and easy to understand. The jargon is explained and the projects cover such things as making cushions and renewing webbing.

GLOSSARY

The glossary at the end of the book gives explanations of some of the technical words and phrases used in the practical sections.

PROFESSIONAL TIPS

All professional cabinetmakers and furniture restorers have their own 'secret' tips, which can save you a considerable amount of time and effort, as well as assist you in the selection of the best tools and equipment for any given job. All the tips included in this book have been provided by successful professional restorers and are the result of their many years of experience in their respective fields. Written in plain language, the tips are included in boxes in the relevant work chapters.

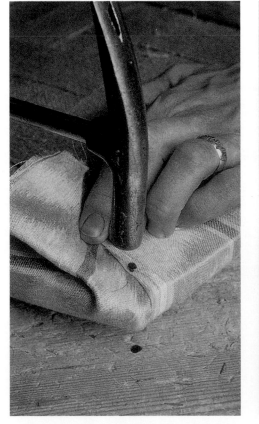

Opposite page
Top left
Cleaning polished wood.
Top right
Stripping old veneer.
Bottom left
Renewing a rush seat.
Bottom right
Making piping for cushions.

This page
Top left
Gilding a shell.
Top right
Repairing a caned seat.
Bottom left
Attaching the covering to a drop-in set.
Bottom right
Making a stitched edge for an overstuffed chair.

Woodwork

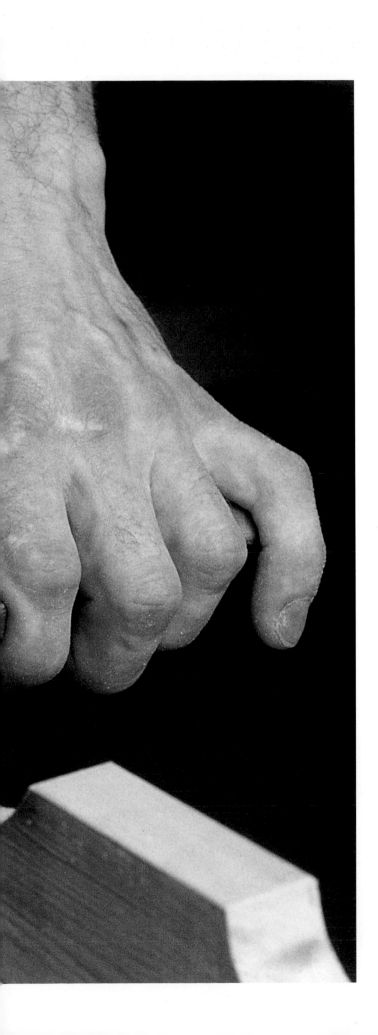

To many people, the words 'restoration' and 'repair' mean the same thing. There is, however, a subtle difference. Repairing a piece of furniture is to mend it so that it is once more serviceable, without consideration of or respect for its original appearance; restoring a piece, on the other hand, means returning it as nearly as possible to its authentic state whilst preserving as much as possible of the patina of the years.

Examination of a piece of old furniture will usually reveal repair or restoration work undertaken at various intervals throughout its life. Such work is not always immediately apparent: for example, the signs of repair on a veneered surface may be merely subtle variations in grain, texture or colour. And whereas mends to broken legs are easy to detect, leg joints can be put back almost invisibly. In extreme cases, some parts - such as the ball feet of a sideboard - may have been removed altogether.

Successful repair and restoration require special tools. There are numerous types of these, and each type appears in many guises. However, although a professional cabinetmaker will usually possess a great number of specialist tools, the beginner can often do satisfactory work with only a limited number. In addition to the traditional hand tools, you can also use electric power tools which can often make a job quicker and easier. But it is as well to be wary of power tools. They may be quicker but they are not necessarily better, are rarely suitable for precision work, and are potentially dangerous.

Cabinetmakers are usually only too willing to give help and advice, particularly if you catch them out of working hours. It is always worth picking their brains to elicit their 'tricks of the trade', to find out how to use special tools, and to discover better ways of using the traditional ones.

Repair and restoration require a patience and skill which improves with experience. A high degree of accuracy and a willingness to become familiar with the technical terms are essential to successful work. Given time, patience and aptitude, anyone can restore a piece of furniture to its former glory.

Left
Making a new top for a dresser. Shown here:
using a spokeshave to tidy up some rough edges
left by a jigsaw.

Types of wood

Timber is bought and sold in many different ways, and there are literally thousands of types of wood. To the novice woodworker, buying timber can be confusing, and the jargon used by merchants does not make matters any simpler.

BUYING TIMBER

High-quality furniture is usually constructed from hardwood, whereas lesser-quality pieces are often made from softwood, or even from manmade boards. Softwood is timber from an evergreen tree like a pine or a spruce. These trees grow comparatively quickly, and consequently their timber is not very dense. Hardwood is timber from a deciduous tree. These trees tend to grow slowly, and consequently their wood is hard, dense and heavy. (Just to confuse matters, balsa is classified as a hardwood even though its timber is light and soft.) Oak, mahogany, teak and walnut are all hardwoods that are commonly used in the construction of furniture. Hardwoods must be seasoned before they are used. Some hardwoods take many years to season thoroughly, and this, of course, adds to the expense of buying them. Hardwood is usually sold rough-sawn in the form of planks or blocks. Of the many manmade boards used to make furniture, plywood, blockboard, MDF and chipboard are the most common. Chipboard, the weakest of the three, is often coated with a layer of melamine or a plastic laminate.

TIMBER MOULDINGS

Mouldings (or beading, as they are sometimes called) are sold in a plethora of different profiles, but it is not always easy to find an exact match for an existing piece –

1 Cherry
2 Cedar
3 Ash
4 Holly
5 Pine
6 Beech
7 Pear
8 Canadian birch
9 Boxwood
10 Chestnut
11 Mahogany
12 Sycamore
13 Lime
14 Maple
15 Walnut
16 Elm
17 Oak
18 Yew

particularly if it is old. This can be very frustrating if you are trying to patch a piece of furniture! If the worst comes to the worst, you may have to commission a timber yard to cut a moulding especially for you. Alternatively, you could shape a length of wood yourself, using a specially shaped plane. When buying mouldings, check that they are straight and that they are free of knots. Knots have the habit of falling out or 'weeping' unless they are treated with a knotting compound first. Mouldings can be of either softwood or hardwood, but hardwood ranges are limited.

VENEERS

Veneers are thin sheets of exotic or decorative wood that are glued onto a groundwork of cheaper wood or manmade board which will not warp or split. Veneering is not a way of making a cheap job look more expensive. Some of the woods used as veneers are rare and expensive, and in some cases the trees themselves are very small or the wood itself is unstable. For these reasons, the woods are not used to make furniture. Occasionally, veneers are let into solid wood in the form of motifs, inlays or strings – this is obviously a

skilful business and requires a great deal of patience. Over the years, veneer-cutting machinery has improved, and veneers have become ever thinner.

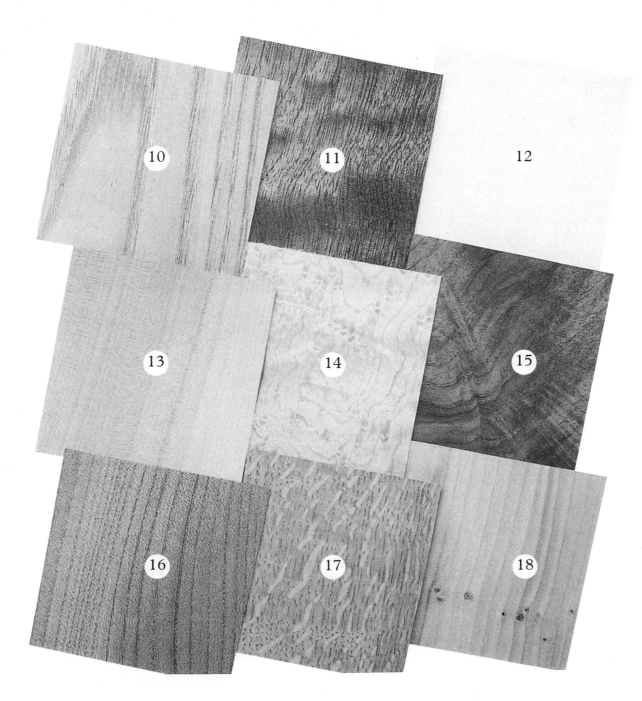

Hand tools

Even the most basic repairs to furniture demand the use of a few tools. Some wood-working tools are highly specialised and are worth buying only if they are applicable to the particular job you are planning. Others can be used in a variety of different projects, and are therefore worth buying at the outset.

ESSENTIAL TOOLS

Discussed here are some of the basic tools you will need. The list could be expanded, and your collection of tools will grow as you gain in confidence and experience.

Screwdrivers are a necessity. It is as well to have a selection of both types, that is, crosshead and flathead.

Saws come in several shapes and sizes. The most useful are a small tenon saw, a coping saw and a panel saw.

Hammers are necessary for tapping home nails and pins. Start with a medium-sized clawhammer and a pin hammer.

An awl looks like a small screwdriver but is in fact designed to start small holes for screws. It is an invaluable gadget.

Chisels are expensive, so choose your first set carefully. Bevel-edged chisels are the best type to opt for as they can be worked in tight corners. Firmer chisels are the alternative, but they are not so versatile.

Clamps (or cramps) are crucial to the cabinetmaker and restorer. In the short run, it is often cheaper to hire, rather than buy, sash clamps, but it is certainly worth purchasing a selection of G-clamps. Web or tourniquet clamps are inexpensive and are useful for holding entire pieces together.

A steel measuring tape and a boxwood rule are used in nearly every job. A square about 12in (30cm) long is a valuable instrument, as is a marking gauge.

A wheelbrace drill is needed for many jobs. The alternative is a brace, but braces are not so accurate, and their use demands more skill.

Planes come in many forms. A smoothing plane is the best type to start off with. For further discussion of planes, see page 15.

Among the miscellaneous tools you will need are sanding blocks, pliers, pincers, a sharpening stone and a rasp or planer file.

Top (left to right)
Marking gauges, Bevel, Try squares (square), Conbination set and Carpentwrs pencils..

Middle
A selection of Wheelbraces and hand drills..

Left (top to bottom)
Awls, Bradawls, Grimltet and a Tacklifter.

Left (top to bottom)
Jack plane, Block planes, Smooth plane and a Spokeshove.

Left
Mallets

BUYING TOOLS

Always buy the best-quality tools you can afford and be particularly wary of plastic and imported tools – they do not wear well.

Electric and special tools

ELECTRIC TOOLS

Traditional cabinetmakers tend to twitch at the very mention of electric tools. However, used in moderation, they can make a job quicker and they take out some of the hard work. Mentioned here are some electric tools that can save you time and effort.

The electric drill is one of the most versatile and universally used tools. If you can afford it, choose a type that has variable speeds and that can be fitted with attachments.

An electric planer will remove enormous amounts of wood very quickly.

An electric router is handy for cutting rebates. The more sophisticated types can be adapted to cut dovetails.

A jigsaw is useful for cutting curved shapes out of sheet materials.

An orbital sander will make light work of rough surfaces. A belt sander is even more efficient.

Electric tools

1 Electric drill
2 Router
3 Electric Planer
4 Cordless screwdriver
5 Heatgun
6 Jigsaw
7 Power saw (circular saw)

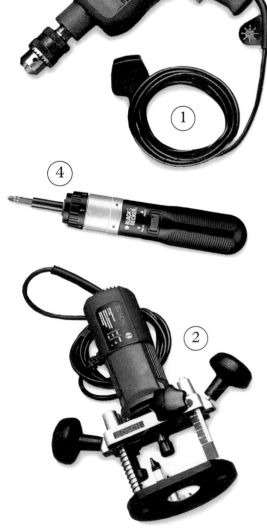

SPECIAL TOOLS

Some restoration work on wooden furniture demands the use of special tools. Of the many available, you may require some of the ones mentioned here.

There are various different types of planes. A shoulder plane is designed to cut across the grain of the wood. A multi-plane, or combination plane, is used for shaping mouldings. Rebate planes can be fitted with different blades; they are designed to cut grooves and rebates in high-quality furniture.

The spokeshave is valuable for many tasks. There are several different types of blade and they can be adapted to shape pieces of wood to suit particular needs. Scraper planes are similar to spokeshaves but are used to remove varnish and paint, rather than wood.

Finally, the cabinet scraper is used to finish timber preparatory to painting or varnishing.

Special tools

1 Rabbet plane

2 Compass plane

3 Router

4 Carving chisels (carving gouges)

5 Dovetail saw

6 Callipers

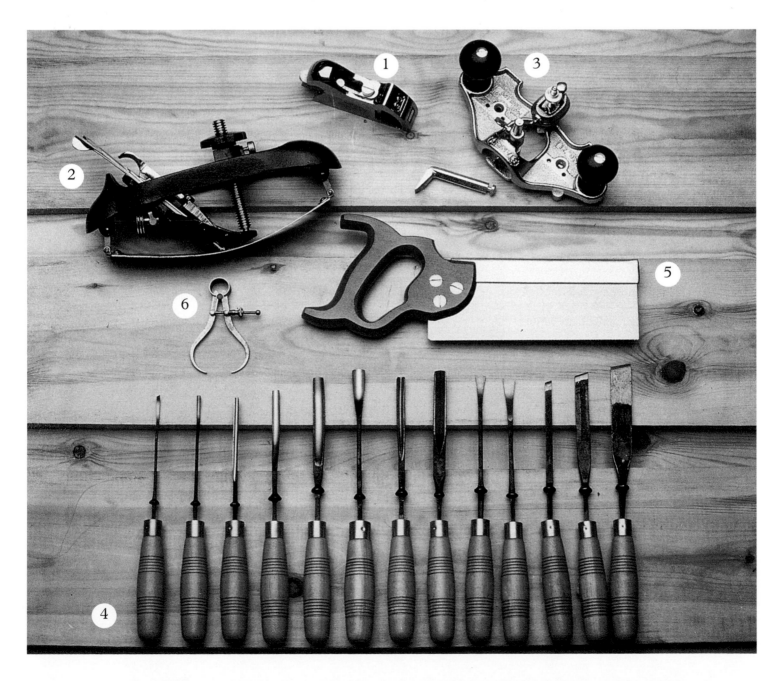

Sharpening and storing tools

Obviously, cutting tools become blunted with use. You can, of course, get them re-sharpened professionally, but it often makes sense to do the job yourself.

SHARPENING A CHISEL OR PLANE

The blades of planes and chisels have much the same shape and profile, so broadly speaking both types of blade are sharpened in exactly the same way. What you need to sharpen a plane or chisel blade are a sharpening stone and plenty of engineering oil; the oil lubricates the movement on the stone and guarantees finesse. If possible, use a dual-stone – these have fine carborundum granules on one side and coarse ones on the other.

When sharpening, start with the coarse-grained side and finish with the other. A sharpening guide is a useful tool to have around – it holds the blade flat and at the correct angle. When sharpening a blade, always try to keep it flat on the stone. Similarly, check that the stone is smooth before you start.

SHARPENING A SAW

The humble panel or tenon saw is perhaps the most elementary carpentry tool, yet it is often abused. Saw teeth are invariably made from a softer metal than is the body of the saw, which is made from a flexible hard steel. Teeth are made from soft steel for a good reason: it makes them easier to sharpen. You might think that toughened teeth could be a good thing – and you can, in fact, buy saws with such teeth – but once they have worn blunt they are rendered virtually useless. In order to sharpen an ordinary saw effectively, you need three pieces of equipment: a saw-setting tool, a file guide and a fine saw file. Armed with these tools you will find saw sharpening is easy.

SHARPENING A PLANE

1 All traces of rust and pitting must be removed from the back of the blade. Do this by placing the blade flat on the stone and working it up and down. Lubricate profusely with oil.

2 Still using the coarse side of the stone, turn the blade over and hold it at an angle of about 25 degrees. Grind the blade until you achieve an even bevel.

3 When you have shaped the edge to your satisfaction, turn over the stone so that you can hone the blade to a keen edge using the fine-grained side. Keep adding oil for lubrication.

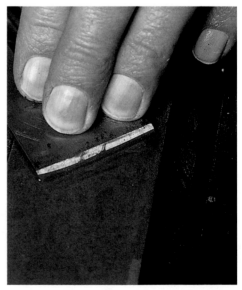

4 As you work the blade up and down the stone, you will notice a burr forming on the reverse side. Remove the burr by rubbing the back of the blade flat against the stone.

USING A SHARPENING GUIDE

A sharpening guide can be adapted to suit both plane and chisel blades. The tool holds the blade at a specific angle while you are manoeuvring it along the sharpening stone.

SETTING A PLANE

Planes are notoriously difficult to set, especially for the beginner. Start by adjusting the angle of depth of the blade – this is usually operated by a wheel on the body of the plane.

Unfortunately, there are no hard-and-fast rules as to how far out the blade should be – it all depends on how much wood you want to lose and what type of wood you are working. However, here are a few guidelines.

● If you want to lose a lot of wood from a softwood, then set the blade deep.

● If you want to lose only a little wood from a softwood, set the blade shallow.

● Hardwoods, with the exception of balsa and a few others, need a more reverential treatment – every shaving has to be shallow otherwise the blade gets stuck in the wood. The other thing to check is the angle of the blade. On most modern planes there is a lever which you use to alter the lateral adjustment.

Judge the alignment of the cutting edge by eye so that it is equal on both sides. Treat each wood as it comes – they all demand different approaches. Experience is your greatest ally, so experiment.

1 Position the cap iron (the top piece) over the blade, leaving ⅛in (3mm) spare.

2 Align one eye with the sole of the plane when setting the angle.

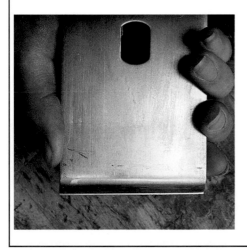

SHARPENING A SCRAPER

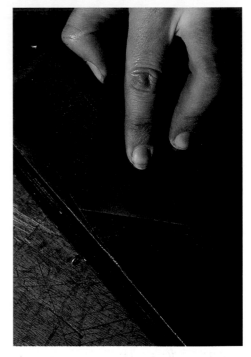

1 The edge of a scraper must be smooth and square before it can be sharpened. Rub the edge of your scraper on the rough side of your sharpening stone to achieve this.

2 Fix the scraper upright in a vice, then run the flat back of a chisel blade over the top to burr over the edge. Use the minimum amount of pressure to assure an even burr.

STORING PLANES

Planes should never be stored with the soleplate flat on a bench. Lay the tool on its side so that the blade cannot get damaged and so that the soleplate itself cannot come into contact with any acids that may seep from the wood of the bench.

SHARPENING DRILL BITS

Certain drill bits are worth re-sharpening yourself. High-speed drills (HSS drills) have bits with toughened-steel cutting edges which are not usually worth tackling unless they are large and therefore expensive to buy. Ordinary bits, however, can be worth re-sharpening. Today, you do not have to have a special grinding wheel to do the job: you can buy electric drill attachments which effectively do the job for you. Look around in your local DIY shop.

Fitting out a workshop

Let it be said at the outset that there is no such thing as the perfect workshop. The best any of us can do is to make the most of what we have available. Many spaces can be adapted. An empty garage, a spare room or a cellar – any of these could be made to suit. But there are certain prerequisites. For a start, a decent and practical workroom must have adequate lighting. This may sound obvious, but many people work away until the early hours of the morning in a badly lit room and then wonder why their work is disappointing: what appears good in poor light invariably turns out to be eye-numbingly bad in the cold light of day. Good electric lighting is essential. If you have the choice, opt for fluorescent lamps. Their light may be ugly but it is also even, and the shadows it casts are not so sharp as to distort your perception of the job in front of you – a major problem with conventional electric lighting.

FINDING THE SPACE

A few – a very few – people manage to create and restore furniture in confined spaces. But most of us like plenty of 'elbow room', in which we can wield a saw or a hammer as the case may be. Of course, much depends on the type of work you are doing, or intend to do, but by and large restorers always want more room than they have available. If you are starting from scratch, there are a few things you should consider from the outset. Good ventilation is paramount, especially if you are going to be handling noxious materials or tools that are likely to create dust. A garage will probably be fine on this count, but a cellar can create problems. Another of your considerations should be the location of power sockets, especially if you intend using electric tools or lighting accessories.

WORKBENCHES

The traditional beechtop workbench from Scandinavia, complete with built-in vices, storage chambers and racks, is hardly a realistic option for most of us. Not only are these benches extremely expensive, they also occupy a great deal of space. However, a stable workbench of some sort is essential. The best type of bench to opt for if you are short of space and cannot afford to lash out on a full-blooded

Above
A collapsible workbench can be a boon if you are short of space.
Right
The workbench in use

bench is a collapsible worktop. There are many types to choose from – most incorporate a clamping system and can withstand a great deal of weight. An alternative is a homemade set-up created from trestles. Be wary of these – they are cheap to erect, but they are also notoriously unstable. An accessory that is well worth considering is a sawhorse. You can either make one from scratch or buy the components in kit form from any of a number of manufacturers.

STORAGE

Before you establish your work area, it is worth considering all the equipment you may want to store – if not right now, then in the future. For example, how do you reckon to keep long lengths of timber so that they stay straight and true? Ideally, timber should be stored flat and straight – it should be supported at regular intervals so that there is no chance of it sagging.

Storing sheets and lengths of timber against a wall will do for a short period, but in time they will inevitably warp and twist. Think about how to store such materials. Remember also that you should keep them in a dry, airy place. An obvious place to store materials is overhead. This arrangement can be fixed up in a garage, in an attic, or even in a spare room. If you do decide on an overhead system, ensure that the supports are both adequately strong and adequately spaced.

Chisels, planes and screwdrivers should be kept vertical. This is easier said than done, but if you have available wall space consider fitting a purpose-built (or factory-made) rack on the wall. In time, you will need storage chests or drawers for items like polish, sharpening stones and all the rest. Consider how to store such items before you commit yourself to the overall layout of your workshop.

Left
If wall space is not available a tool roll will keep chisels safe.

Adhesives, abrasives and finishes

ADHESIVES

It is important for the restorer to use the right glue for the job in hand, bearing in mind the various properties of certain glues.

Animal glue is the traditional cabinetmaker's adhesive. It comes in toffee-like sheets or granules named 'pearls'. The pearls should be soaked overnight and subsequently heated in a double container (*bain-marie*). Although difficult to use, this type of glue has the advantage of being reactivated by heat – an invaluable property if you are veneering.

PVA (white woodworker's adhesive) is readily available and is comparatively cheap. Synthetic-resin adhesives come in two parts: a thick, syrupy liquid, and a hardener. These adhesives are immensely strong but they are awkward to handle. They are best for joints that can be clamped together. When handling these adhesives, take heed of the manufacturer's instructions.

Uraldehyde glues come in the form of a powder that has to be mixed with water. These adhesives are strong and slow-setting, which makes them suitable for many purposes. But, once set, they are set for good!

Contact adhesives are commonplace. From the cabinetmaker's point of view, they have little value, but for quick, necessary repairs to many manmade materials they are unsurpassed for strength and durability.

Epoxy adhesives are renowned for their strength, but they are best kept for minor repairs because they are tricky to use on large areas.

Superglues are comparatively new. They are seldom appropriate for furniture restoration. Glue guns may be terrific if you are laying tiles in your house, but for furniture they are only really useful for gimping in upholstery. Glue film has highly specialised uses and is very expensive: it is used specifically for laying on veneers.

ABRASIVES

Abrasive papers are available in a number of grit sizes (an indication of roughness) and are made from a variety of abrasive materials.

Garnet paper is usually the coarsest type and is covered with an orange-coloured grit. Aluminium-oxide paper is often grey in colour;

ADHESIVES FOR WOOD						
TYPE OF GLUE	STRESS RESISTANCE	WATER RESISTANCE	DAMP RESISTANCE	MOULD RESISTANCE	GAP-FILLING PROPERTIES	LIABLE TO STAIN
Uraldehyde glues	excellent	good	good	good	excellent	yes
PVA	good	good	good	fair	good	no
Animal glues	excellent	poor	poor	fair	poor	no
Resin and epoxy	excellent	excellent	excellent	excellent	excellent	yes
Contact glues	good	excellent	excellent	excellent	good	yes
'Superglues'	poor	good	good	excellent	poor	yes
Glue guns	poor	good	good	poor	poor	no

FINISHES FOR WOOD					
TYPES OF FINISH	SOFTWOOD	HARDWOOD	DRYING TIME (HOURS)	NUMBER OF COATS	APPLICATION
Wood stain	good	poor	4	2-3	brush
Varnish	good	good	12	2-3	brush
Lacquer	good	good	4	2-3	brush
Wax polish	good	excellent	1	several	cloth
French polish	fair	superb	24	10-15	cloth

it is commonly used with orbital sanders. Silicon-carbide paper is often referred to as 'wet-and-dry' paper; it is rarely used in woodwork, but is useful for cleaning metal parts.

FINISHES

There are many different types of finishes available and they are not all are compatible with each other.

French polish is a solution of shellac in alcohol. The alcohol evaporates, leaving a thin coating of shellac on the surface of the piece of furniture. Usually several coats of French polish are applied, and it is common to finish off with a wax polish. The best wax polishes contain beeswax but, because this is hard in its natural state, it is nearly always mixed with synthetic waxes to make the resultant polish easier to apply.

Polyurethane varnish can be applied to give a high-gloss or semi-matte finish. It is tough and hard-wearing, but it is not suitable for use on good-quality furniture. Cellulose lacquers can be coloured, as can French polish. Like polyurethane varnishes, lacquers are durable.

Also, there are several types of stains for colouring wood preparatory to polishing. Several grades of abrasive paper are needed to obtain a good surface. Start with a coarse paper and move on to finer and finer papers – always working with the grain.

Abrasives
1 Garnet papers (orange)
2 Aluminium oxide (black or grey)
3 Silicone carbide (wet and dry)

Nails and screws

Nails are rarely used in furniture-making, except sometimes at the lower end of the market. Panel pins and veneer pins, however, are used extensively to fasten backs onto cabinets and drawer bottoms onto drawer backs and to hold mouldings in place while the glue sets. Veneer (or moulding) pins are made from very fine wire and are easily bent, especially when they are inserted into hardwoods. Hardboard pins have a square section and are often copper-plated to protect against corrosion. Panel pins are a larger version of veneer pins and come in several different sizes.

Screws come in three head types: countersunk, roundhead and raised head, and they have either a slot or a cross on top which enables them to be driven into the wood. Screws are available in a variety of lengths and gauges. These gauges start at 2 (the thinnest) and go upwards in even numbers to 20 (the thickest). The sizes most commonly used in furniture making are 2, 4, 6, 8 and 10.

As far as furniture is concerned, only brass and steel screws are important. Of the two metals, brass is softer and so screws made of this metal should be handled with care.

Chipboard screws are different from ordinary wood screws in that the shank is parallel instead of tapered and the thread is a double spiral rather than a single spiral.

NAIL AND PIN TYPES

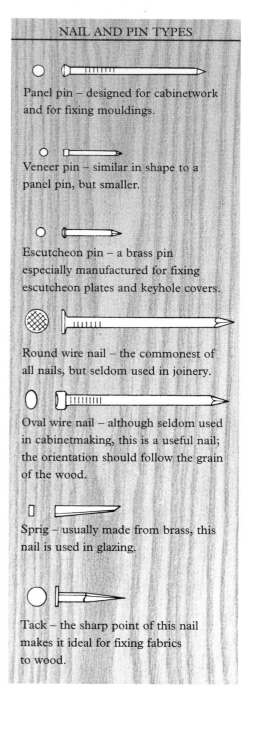

Panel pin – designed for cabinetwork and for fixing mouldings.

Veneer pin – similar in shape to a panel pin, but smaller.

Escutcheon pin – a brass pin especially manufactured for fixing escutcheon plates and keyhole covers.

Round wire nail – the commonest of all nails, but seldom used in joinery.

Oval wire nail – although seldom used in cabinetmaking, this is a useful nail; the orientation should follow the grain of the wood.

Sprig – usually made from brass, this nail is used in glazing.

Tack – the sharp point of this nail makes it ideal for fixing fabrics to wood.

USING PANEL PINS

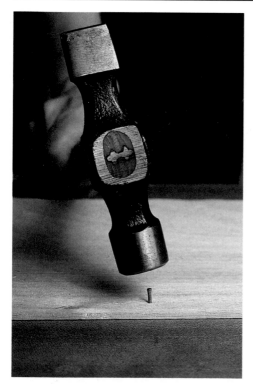

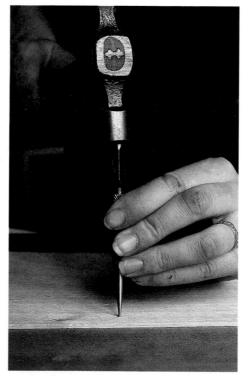

1 Panel pins should be tapped home gently – they are easy to bend.

2 Use a nail punch to sink the head below the surface of the wood.

TYPES

Screws are available in brass, steel, copper, aluminium and gunmetal. They can have black-japanned, galvanised, tin-nickel- or chromium-plated finishes. They are measured from head to tip and the gauge is defined by the diameter of the shank.

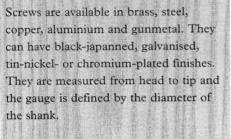

Screws have two slot types: straight-slot (1) and crosshead (2). Special screwdrivers are required for driving certain crosshead screws.

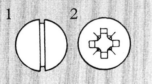

Screws are also available in three basic shapes; countersunk (3) screws are designed to lie beneath the surface of the wood; roundhead (4) screws leave the crown above the surface; raised-head (5) screws are a cross between the two – the top of this is visible but not too obvious.

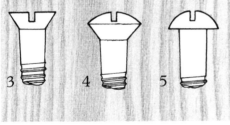

DRIVING SCREWS

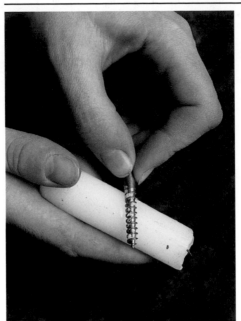

1 To prevent a steel screw from sticking, rub it over a candle.

2 Drill a pilot hole for the screw, then countersink the hole with a special bit.

3 Be sure to use the correct type and size of screwdriver.

4 Once it has been driven home, the head of the screw should lie beneath the surface.

Fittings

The range of hinges, locks, catches and stays is now so huge that even professional cabinet-makers cannot keep up with it. The simple butt hinge of yesteryear has been transformed into a multiplicity of 'triumphs of engineering', as applied to modern kitchen units!

HINGES AND STAYS

There are literally hundreds of different types of hinges. As far as furniture is concerned, butt hinges are the most frequently used. They are used to hang doors and they come in many different sizes to suit most jobs. A variation on the butt hinge is the piano hinge, which is considerably longer. The backflap hinge is also a butt hinge, but it has wider leaves and is used in drop-leaf tables where greater strength is required.

Stays are used on fall-front bureaux and on the dropdoors of drinks cabinets. The traditional cranked stay has been largely superseded by the sliding stay, which is more efficient.

LOCKS

Locks come in a variety of designs. The commonest type is the mortise lock, large versions of which can be found in many doors. Small mortise locks are suitable for drawers and cabinets. You should have little trouble in finding a size to suit any particular job you have in mind. More specialised locks include the piano mortise lock, which has a bolt that moves both upwards and sideways.

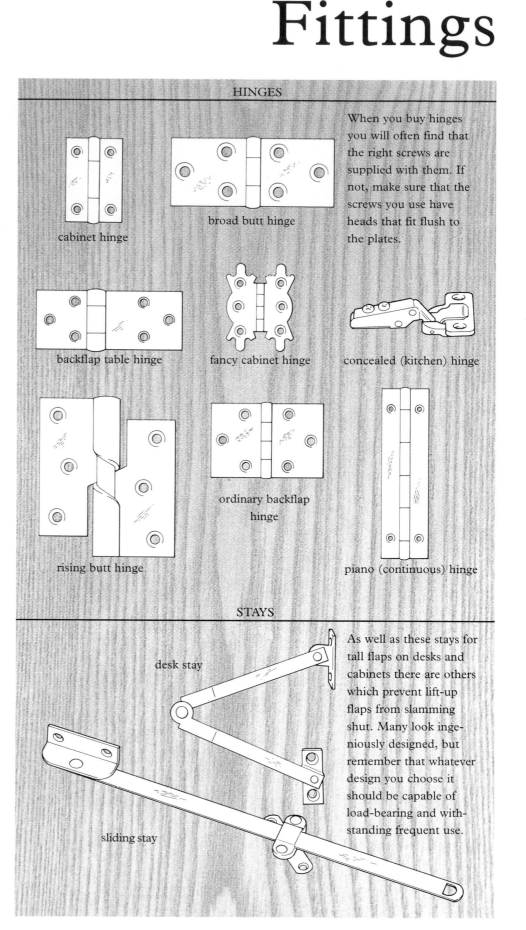

HINGES

cabinet hinge

broad butt hinge

When you buy hinges you will often find that the right screws are supplied with them. If not, make sure that the screws you use have heads that fit flush to the plates.

backflap table hinge

fancy cabinet hinge

concealed (kitchen) hinge

rising butt hinge

ordinary backflap hinge

piano (continuous) hinge

STAYS

desk stay

sliding stay

As well as these stays for tall flaps on desks and cabinets there are others which prevent lift-up flaps from slamming shut. Many look ingeniously designed, but remember that whatever design you choose it should be capable of load-bearing and withstanding frequent use.

CORNERS

Brass corners not only add strength to certain pieces of furniture, they also look good. They are traditionally used on military chests, but there is no reason not to use them on small boxes as well. They are available in many sizes, and are often sold complete with screws. Corners can be plain or fancy – the choice is yours. You can also get corners made of steel, but these are not always as attractive.

If you want to add strength to a corner but do not want any brace to be visible, you can buy internal corners. These are sometimes tricky to fit, but they do guarantee a sturdy piece of furniture.

CASTORS

Castors can have large or small wheels, with or without tyres. Some are mounted on plates that are screwed to the underside of the legs of a piece of furniture; others have spigots that are inserted into the legs. Of the two types, those with spigots tend to be stronger, but they are more difficult to fit – it is tricky to drill the holes for the spigots accurately.

Castors can be bought in several sizes, and there are many patented designs. When you buy, bear in mind that some castors can detract from the look of a piece of furniture. They are not attractive accessories, so think twice before you decide to fit them.

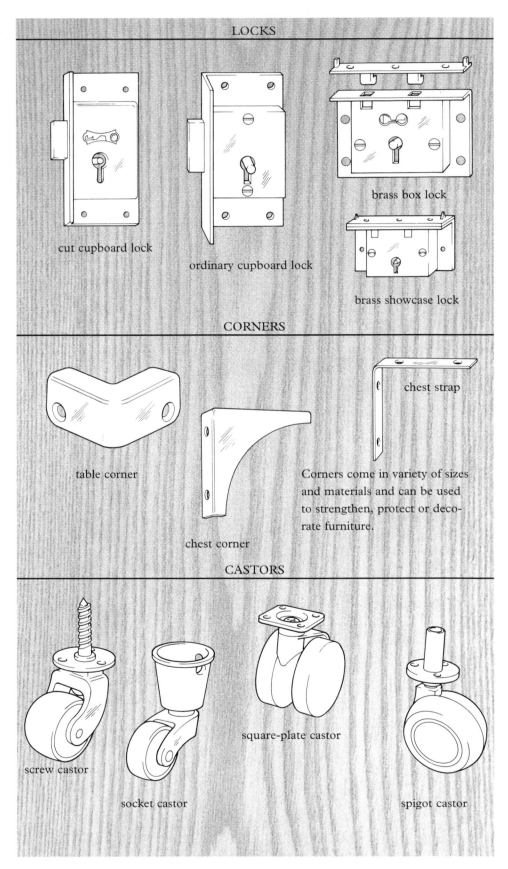

LOCKS

cut cupboard lock

ordinary cupboard lock

brass box lock

brass showcase lock

CORNERS

table corner

chest corner

chest strap

Corners come in variety of sizes and materials and can be used to strengthen, protect or decorate furniture.

CASTORS

screw castor

socket castor

square-plate castor

spigot castor

Isolating weak points

Faults in furniture can be divided into two groups: structural and superficial. In pieces of furniture composed mainly of frames, such as chairs and tables, the commonest faults include loose joints, broken legs, broken rails, damaged corners and missing parts, such as decorative moulding.

CHAIRS

Chairs suffer a greater variety of problems than any other piece of furniture, simply because they are open to more abuse – people stand on them and often tilt them onto their back legs.

The weak points are inevitably the joints which hold the legs to the seat – if these become loose the chair will wobble. It is worth remembering that most traditionally made chairs are held together by glue alone, and in most cases this glue is brittle and inflexible. In other words, if the glue cracks, there is little that can be done to help stability other than dismantling the chair and rebuilding it using fresh adhesive.

Arms and spindles on certain types of chair are also vulnerable, and again the best way of curing weak joints is to strip them down, clean them up and reassemble them.

Luckily, the joints on most chairs are straightforward and are fairly easy to strip down.

TABLES

Generally speaking, tables are more susceptible to superficial faults than to structural ones – the legs tend to get kicked and scratched and the top is liable to get things dropped or spilled on it.

Superficial repairs to tables can demand a great deal of skill and, especially, patience. Perhaps one of the most difficult and frustrating things to tackle is getting rid of heat rings made by a hot pan being laid on the table. There is a lot to be said for the old maxim: prevention is better than cure. Once you have restored a table, protect its surface, especially from hot pans and pots.

The joints found in tables can be surprisingly complicated – for example, mortise and tenon joints are often cross-doweled for extra strength. Should they come loose, these joints can be difficult to repair.

CHESTS AND CABINETS

A cabinet is essentially a box into which either drawers or doors are fitted. It is with cabinets that the skilled workmanship of the craftsman is most often to be found. The joints tend to be complicated and are therefore difficult to strip down. On the other hand, they are less likely to have come apart in the first place! It is worth noting that you should never take a cabinet apart completely unless it is absolutely necessary: it usually requires a certain amount of violence to separate glued parts, and this can make matters worse rather than better.

Cabinets and chests are often veneered and often sport decorative mouldings. Of all the things that you are likely to have to repair on a cabinet these are the commonest. However, broken hinges and damaged drawer-runners are also frequently encountered.

WEAK POINTS TO LOOK FOR – CHAIRS

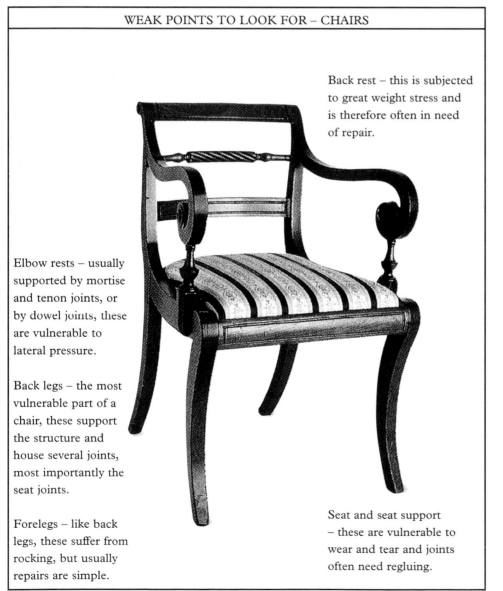

Back rest – this is subjected to great weight stress and is therefore often in need of repair.

Elbow rests – usually supported by mortise and tenon joints, or by dowel joints, these are vulnerable to lateral pressure.

Back legs – the most vulnerable part of a chair, these support the structure and house several joints, most importantly the seat joints.

Forelegs – like back legs, these suffer from rocking, but usually repairs are simple.

Seat and seat support – these are vulnerable to wear and tear and joints often need regluing.

WEAK POINTS TO LOOK FOR – TABLES

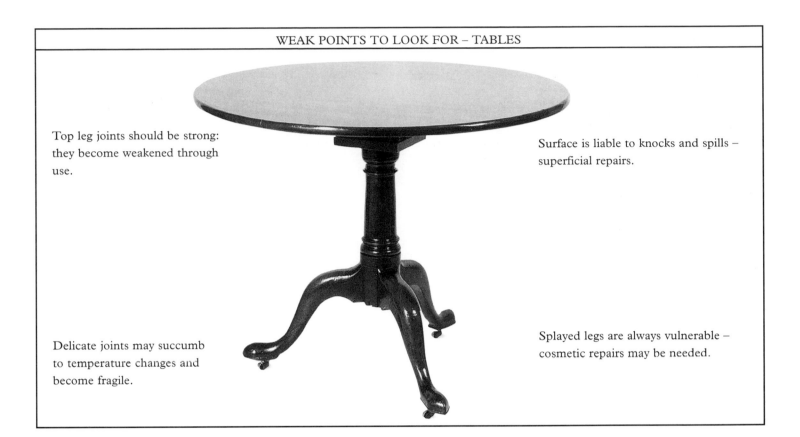

Top leg joints should be strong: they become weakened through use.

Delicate joints may succumb to temperature changes and become fragile.

Surface is liable to knocks and spills – superficial repairs.

Splayed legs are always vulnerable – cosmetic repairs may be needed.

WEAK POINTS TO LOOK FOR – CABINETS

Superficial scratches and dents are often found.

Corner joints are often subjected to strain and may need strengthening.

Stains – these can be a problem on work tables; subtle remedies are called for.

Legs and supports are subject to scuffing – cosmetic treatment is required.

Tackling woodworm and rot

Woodworm and rot are the bane of many households. Although woodworm is found in nearly every home, thankfully it can be easily treated and the tell-tale holes covered up. Dry rot, however, is not so easily dealt with, and drastic measures are usually called for.

WOODWORM

You are unlikely ever to see a living woodworm (or common furniture beetle), as these creatures are dull brown in colour and only about ⅛in (3mm) long. The eggs are laid in summer in small cracks in the woodwork or in existing woodworm holes. The grubs hatch after six weeks or so and spend the next year or two eating their way through the wood. Then they pupate, tunnel their way to the surface and fly away as adults to start the cycle all over again.

Attacks are usually on the backs of furniture or under framing; pieces should be checked periodically for any sign of the fine dust that betrays worm activity. If you spot any symptoms of woodworm, take action immediately. Run a vacuum cleaner over the surface to remove dust from the holes, then inject each hole with woodworm-killer. Swab the surface liberally with the fluid, taking all the precautions advised by the manufacturer.

If you detect woodworm in upholstered pieces of furniture, you may find that you have to remove the upholstery from the affected area before you can treat the infected timber.

DRY ROT

Dry rot is a fungus that breaks up wood into crumbling cubes. Contrary to its name, it thrives in damp conditions. It has a very distinctive fungal smell and can travel like wildfire through any other wood nearby. Furniture that is kept in a damp cellar can be contaminated.

Dry rot is not often found in free-standing furniture, but, when it does appear, it must be dealt with immediately. Affected wood must be cut out and burned. Sound timber should be treated with one of the proprietary preservatives recommended for the purpose. These chemicals are necessarily highly toxic and so great care should be taken when using them. Always read the instructions carefully and carry them out to the letter.

TREATING WOODWORM

1 Treat outbreaks of woodworm infestation with a proprietary woodworm fluid. Flood each hole separately, using the nozzle on the can as a guide. Aerosols are available for this. Wear gloves for safety.

2 As a preventative measure, wipe the fluid over the rest of the piece of furniture – this will deter adult beetles from laying eggs in cracks or holes.

The existence of only a few worm holes in the surface does not mean that the damage is minimal – the inside may be badly affected. Replace seriously damaged parts with new wood if a liquid wood-hardener does not restore the timber's strength.

PREVENTING WOODWORM INFESTATION AND DRY ROT

There are several things you can do to prevent woodworm attacks.

● Treat any new timber additions, such as mouldings or spindles, with a proprietary woodworm fluid before you fix them in place. Once the fluid has dried it can be stained and polished in the usual way.

● If you do not want to paint a piece of furniture, you can buy special waxes which contain an insecticide. These polishes are an effective deterrent against woodworm but, to get the maximum benefit, you need to apply them regularly.

● Dry rot flourishes only in damp conditions, so if you are storing pieces of furniture make sure the place is dry. Do not be tempted to wrap furniture up in plastic sheeting – this will make the timber sweat.

COSMETIC REPAIRS TO WOODWORM DAMAGE

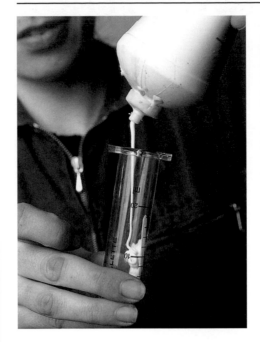

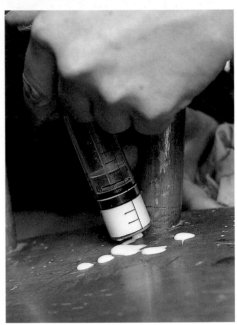

1 Woodworm holes can be filled with ordinary PVA adhesive. This can be easily applied using a syringe.

2 Inject the adhesive into the woodworm holes. Wipe off excess adhesive with a damp rag and then leave the glue to dry hard; this should take only an hour or two.

3 When the adhesive has set, rub stopping compound (sometimes called Brummer paste) over the holes. This will disguise and camouflage them.

4 When the stopping compound has dried, polish the furniture to complete the repair. If you want extra protection, use a special insecticidal polish.

Cleaning furniture

Before a piece of furniture can be examined properly for faults, it should first be cleaned.

Be prepared to spend time cleaning – a chair, for example, could take at least a day to clean thoroughly. Often the most time-consuming part is getting grime and accumulated dirt out of nooks and crannies. It is worth doing this, however, because it is surprising how much they show up if you have neglected to deal with them. Try and determine the difference between a build-up of dirt and desirable patination: this can affect the value of a piece if you decide to sell it.

If the piece of furniture has metal parts, be sure to remove them before you start work on them.

TOOLS AND MATERIALS
For cleaning painted surfaces:
- warm, soapy water
- a soft cloth
- a stiff brush (a toothbrush is ideal)

For cleaning polished wood:
- a reviving fluid – 4 parts linseed oil, 4 parts turpentine, 4 parts white vinegar, and 1 part methylated spirits – works well; alternatively, use a proprietary cleaning fluid
- a toothbrush

CLEANING PAINTED SURFACES

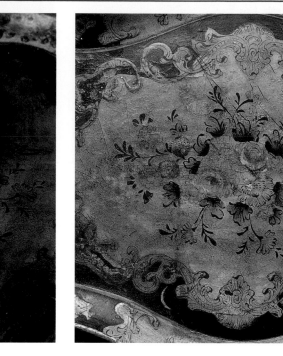

1 Work soapy water over the surface. Be sure not to flood the workpiece.

2 Wipe the surface clean using a new cloth, which should be clean and dry.

CLEANING POLISHED WOOD

1 Work the reviving fluid over the surface and into corners and mouldings.

2 Wipe off the fluid as quickly as possible so that there is no chance of it damaging the wood. Use a toothbrush to clean intricate mouldings and awkward corners.

For cleaning and burnishing metal:
- proprietary rust-remover
- burnishing paste
- light engineering oil
- protective gloves
- a stiff brush
- 0000 gauge steel wool
- a cloth

CLEANING WOOD

The essential thing to remember when cleaning wood is that you want to remove only the dirt, not the polish or paint underneath it. In other words, be gentle. Soapy water works wonders with grease and dust, but if you want to remove dull coatings of wax mixed with grime, a homemade reviving fluid (see above) works better. There are several proprietary cleaning fluids on the market. The best advice when using one of these is to follow the manufacturer's instructions. Whichever solution you use, it is important not to flood the workpiece – this can lead to blistering.

If you are cleaning carved or intricate pieces of wood, a stiff - but not abrasive - brush is a good tool to have to hand. Use it gently so that you do not scratch the surface of the wood.

CLEANING AND BURNISHING METAL

Steel hinges, locks and handles inevitably get rusty in time. The best way to remove rust is with a proprietary rust-remover. Be sure to wear gloves when handling one of these fluids because they are caustic and can irritate the skin. If you are dealing with something small, like a hinge, it is always best to remove it from the workpiece before you start work.

Once you have removed all traces of rust, work the piece of metal over with a wad of 0000 gauge steel wool. This will get rid of pitting. To get a good shine, use a burnishing paste and then metal polish – this works particularly well on brass and copper.

USING RUST-REMOVER

1 Before handling a rust-remover, put on gloves. Brush the fluid over the workpiece.

2 After 20 minutes or so, wash the fluid off the metal and polish with steel wool.

BURNISHING

1 Wipe off the dirt and grime. Use a brush to get into creases.

2 Work over the piece with fine steel wool and a little light engineering oil.

3 Rub over the surface with fresh steel wool. Use burnishing paste for a clean shine.

Superficial repairs: solid wood

Wooden furniture can be damaged in hundreds of different ways, but some are more common than others. Dents, splits, scratches, burns and stains are perhaps the commonest superficial repairs. When dealing with such a repair, it is easy to think that just because it is superficial it will be easy to tackle. Alas, this is seldom the case. Above all else, be prepared to take time effecting a superficial repair.

STRAIGHTENING BOARDS

Timber is notorious for warping, or 'moving', as the professionals call it. Moisture is usually the culprit. If dry wood gets damp – even only slightly – it expands. This expansion may not, at first, be perceptible to the eye, being recognised only when the wood bends and buckles. Flat boards tend to expand laterally, and bend only when they cannot expand laterally any more. In other words, if a piece of wood is held firmly by joints, it has no option but to buckle.

Straightening a warped piece of timber requires both special skill and special equipment, and for this reason you are advised to seek out a professional.

SPLITS

Very slight splits can be cleaned out and re-glued, but if the split is much more than a hairline crack this treatment will not work because the pressure exerted by the wood will open up the wound again. If the split is wide, it should be filled with a sliver of shaped, matching wood.

PREVENTING SPLITS

Central heating does little for good furniture. All wood contains a certain amount of moisture, which is necessary to keep it stable. If the water is made to evaporate – for example, by central heating – the timber will shrink, and this will lead to cracks and splits. Keep furniture, especially if it is old and mature, away from radiators and other heating appliances. Similarly, good pieces of furniture should not be kept in humid areas like a bathroom or kitchen.

Use PVA adhesive – which is relatively flexible – when effecting such a repair. When you clamp up a split, be sure not to overtighten the clamps: if you do, the pressure may cause one face to rise above the other.

DENTS

The longer a dent has existed in a piece of wood, the harder it is to lift it. Dents in softwoods are the easiest to repair; large dents in hardwoods are the most difficult, and can prove impossible.

Dents caused physically – for example, by dropping something onto a tabletop – are tricky to deal with because fibres in the wood have been broken. A scar of some sort will almost always be left.

Dents caused by hot implements can almost always be levelled. A hot pan placed on a table will cause moisture in the wood to evaporate. This will leave a dent, but the moisture can always be put back in again.

STEAMING DENTS

1 Clean up around the dent before you start any treatment.

2 Place a droplet of water over the dent and allow it to settle.

3 Apply the tip of a soldering iron or a heated screwdriver to the bubble of water.

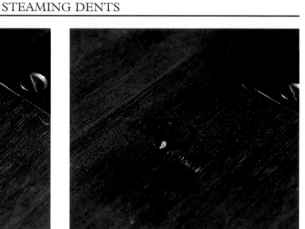

4 When the water has been absorbed and the dent levelled, apply wax.

SCRATCHES

Shallow scratches and scuffs which penetrate the surface of the wood are best filled with wax. You can buy coloured-wax sticks which can be matched to the colour of the wood. Melt the wax into the scratch using a cigarette lighter or a match and scrape it level while the wax is still soft. Buff over the repair when the wax has set hard.

Deep scratches and nicks can also be filled with wax, but they should be tinted back to the surface colour – that is, the colour of the wood – before they are levelled. Wood stains that are guaranteed to be miscible with wax can be used to tint the wax itself – always follow the manufacturer's advice.

BURNS

Burns can range from a light scorching to deep charring.

Scorches can be removed by rubbing over the surface with fine (0000 gauge) steel wool and methyl alcohol. Once you have done this, apply polish.

Deep charring has to be scraped out. The best weapon to use is a round-ended knife that is not too sharp. Having scraped out the worst of the damage, smooth the dent down with fine abrasive paper. Fill the resulting depression with shellac. You can buy shellac in sticks (just like wax).

When you melt shellac into a dent, use a smokeless flame; smoke can discolour shellac. Polish the repair as soon as the shellac has set.

STAINS

Rings left by water or alcohol on the bottom of glasses can often be removed by buffing firmly with wax polish. If this does not work, try wiping over the mark with a cloth dampened with methyl alcohol: this often does the trick. If these methods fail, use a light abrasive. Cigarette ash mixed with linseed oil is almost guaranteed to work. If even this fails, use a burnishing paste gently and work away until the stain disappears. Finish off with a polish which contains wax.

Certain stains, like ink stains, demand special treatment – bleaching. A table that has been well polished should be impervious to ink, but bare wood is always vulnerable.

BLEACHING OUT STAINS

1 Apply diluted bleach to the end of a dowel or match stalk curled with cotton wool.

2 Wearing gloves, dab the bleach over the stain in a circular motion.

3 Give the bleach time to neutralise the stain: about half an hour.

4 Once the bleach has done its work, touch up the woodwork and finish with polish.

Superficial repairs: veneered work

Veneering is the art of gluing thin sheets of expensive, and perhaps exotic, wood onto a base of cheaper wood or, alternatively, a manmade board. Because they are thin and glued, veneers are vulnerable to damage.

BLISTERED VENEER

Blisters can appear on veneer for several reasons. It may be that the fixing glue has weakened over the years, with the consequence that the wood has risen up in rebellion; or it may be that a hot object has been placed on the veneer, thereby causing the base glue to melt and so giving the veneer freedom to move. However, the most likely cause is that the veneer and the basework have contracted in different ways, making the veneer – the thinnest of skins – warp, buckle and blister.

Curing blistered veneer is surprisingly basic in principle – all one has to do is smooth the skin and introduce an adhesive strong enough to hold it down.

CRACKED AND DENTED VENEER

Dents in veneer can be treated in much the same way as similar wounds to solid wood – in other words, they can be steamed. However, if you steam veneer you always run the risk of melting the glue beneath, and this can cause headaches.

A crack along a veneered surface can be reduced by heating it with an iron to soften the glue beneath. Once the glue has been softened the veneer itself can be stretched to bridge the gap. The best tool for this is a special veneering hammer.

PATCHING VENEERED CORNERS

Veneer is easily broken off corners, especially on drawer fronts. Almost always a jagged edge is left behind. The only satisfactory way to tackle such a problem is to shape a new piece of veneer to fit. Trace an outline of the damaged piece onto a sheet of paper. Transfer this shape onto a sheet of matching veneer, cut it out and glue it into place.

One thing to remember is that the surfaces of the basework and veneer should both be completely clean and free from dust.

DEALING WITH BLISTERED VENEER

1 Blisters on old veneer can often be suppressed by applying heat from an iron.

2 Modify a syringe in order to insert PVA adhesive. Two airholes are essential.

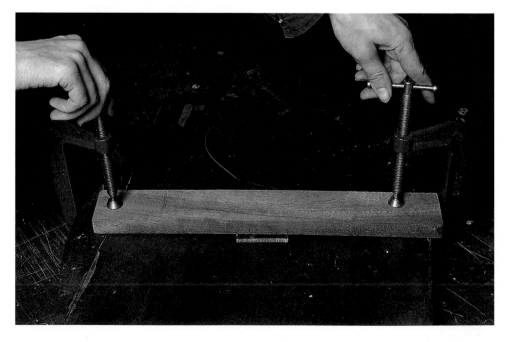

3 Hold down the blister with clamps, making sure to protect the wood from the clamp edges with pieces of wood. If necessary, straddle distances with battens.

STRIPPING OLD VENEER

1 In severe cases, damaged veneer cannot be restored and has to be stripped off. Use an iron to soften old animal glue. A little water on the surface sometimes helps.

2 As the glue softens, slide a palette knife or chisel blade underneath the veneer.

3 Strip off the old veneer and clean up the residue of old glue with hot water.

LAYING NEW VENEER

1 Stretch out the new piece of veneer and tape it down flat.

2 Make a template of the area to be covered and transfer it to the veneer.

5 Use a veneer hammer (or other soft hammer) to beat the veneer smooth. Start in the centre of the repair and work towards the edges to get rid of excess adhesive.

3 Brush a coat of thin animal glue over the surface of the panel.

4 Lay the sheet of prepared veneer over the panel and smooth it out with an iron.

Advanced repairs: veneered work

Re-laying whole pieces of veneer is simple when compared to laying patches in the middle of a piece of furniture. For a start, the cutting has to be accurate, and it is also important that the colours and types of veneer match up perfectly. Obviously enough, small patches can be disguised, but large repairs cannot.

The greatest test of a furniture restorer's ability is whether he or she can match large pieces of veneer, not just for colour and texture, but also for level and tightness of bond.

It may seem obvious enough to most people, but many of us forget the importance of matching veneers. To many, mahogany automatically matches mahogany, but this is, in fact, seldom true. To continue with mahogany as an example, there are many species of this tree – some grow in Africa, others in South America. Most old mahogany furniture was created from the African species, but most 'modern' mahogany, or

---

INSETTING A SMALL VENEER INSERT

1 Mark out the area of a damaged veneer, preferably with a piece of chalk.

2 Cut out the damaged piece with a sharp chisel or knife.

3 Lift up the damaged veneer with a chisel or knife blade.

4 Make a template of the cut-out and transfer this to the new veneer.

5 Prepare the surface with animal glue, filling up any dents or holes.

6 Firm the new section in place, squeezing out glue as you go. Wipe off excess glue.

'bastard' mahogany, as it is sometimes called, comes from South America. It is hardly surprising that the two species do not necessarily match up when they are paired.

The moral of all this is check the colour, quality and thickness of a veneer before you start placing it on a valued piece of furniture. And always remember to align the grain before you stick it into place.

REPLACING VENEER

When you buy sheets of veneer you will probably be surprised, and perhaps disappointed, that they are not flat, shiny, complete pieces of wood. Far from it – you will most probably receive something resembling an overgrown potato crisp. To flatten a potato-crisp veneer, brush it over with warm water and 'squeeze' it between two sheets of damp, warm plywood (use G-clamps to hold the sheets of plywood together). Leave the veneer overnight and it should be flat in the morning.

Once flattened, veneer should be used as quickly as possible, as otherwise it will return to its original shape. If a sheet of veneer starts to resemble a crisp once more, treat it again with the method described above.

If you try to cut untreated veneer it will almost certainly shatter – do not forget that it is not only thin but also extremely brittle.

When you cut veneer, always use a sharp knife. A handyman's knife is a good option, but a scalpel is even better. You can get scalpels – and packets of replaceable blades – quite readily from most art stores.

When cutting sheets of veneer, be sure that you do so on a flat, yet receptive, board. The kitchen table is often ideal . . . but this is not usually a good idea!

MODERN VENEERING METHODS

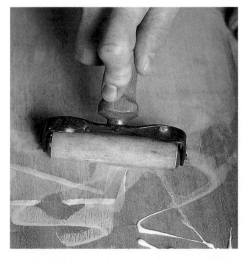

1 Prepare the surface thoroughly before laying the veneer. Use abrasive paper to get rid of lumps and bumps.

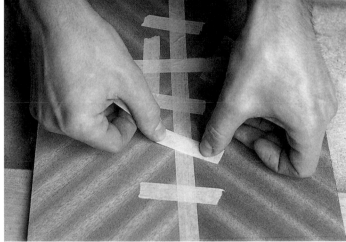

2 If you are laying several sheets of veneer, or plan a mosaic effect, tape the sheets together (masking tape is best) before laying it.

3 Spread adhesive over the surface and roll it into an even coating. Wipe away any excess adhesive.

4 Use a soft roller to get the pieces flat. If you do not have a roller, a soft cloth will do. Start in the middle and work outwards.

Restoring decorative veneers

'Marquetry', 'parquetry', 'lines', 'inlays' and 'strings' – all of these are semi-technical words that refer to decorative veneers (see Glossary). Of course, the sophisticated professional knows these terms off pat. These techniques are found only in high-quality work. To the veneering craftsman they can be the dream, the ultimate test of craft. So if you are considering repairing such work do not go into it in a happy-go-lucky frame of mind.

If you want to replace an entire design, either because you do not like it (hesitate before you act!), or because it has been damaged out of all recognition, you may be able to find 'standard works' to fit. These are obtainable from certain companies and societies, which often advertise in the specialised press.

If you want to create or repair from scratch, respect the woods you deal with.

MATCHING SHAPES

Presented with a panel that is partly damaged, first consider its construction. Some panels are made up of strings that form outlines and details; other panels contain whole sections of coloured wood which build up a mosaic. Needless to say, it is easier to replace a section of whole wood than it is to cut minuscule sections to fit.

If you have a piece of inlaid work that has 'risen', first determine the extent of the damage – it may go beyond the obvious – and, second, consider its shape and colour. In nearly every case, you will find an appropriate string or edge at which the damage ends – this perimeter should form the edge of your repairs. Lift up the damaged pieces (using hot water to melt the glue if necessary). Make a template of the damaged area; anchored tracing paper and a soft pencil are your best options.

USING STRINGING

Strings are essentially narrow inlays set into solid wood. You can readily buy decorative strings which have designs stained into them, and you can also get plain strings. Of course, the ultimate option is to make your own strings, in which case you should consider the type of wood (beech is a common option because it is relatively pliable), the thickness of the string (too thin and it becomes brittle; too thick and it becomes unwieldy) and the colour of the wood. If you are replacing a complete string, you have a wide choice of designs and colours; if you have to match a string, then you must be careful.

LAYING MOTIFS

Laying motifs – or, rather, relaying motifs if you are truly restoring – can cause problems. Motifs are often special – not necessarily to you, but most probably to the person who laid them or to the person who commissioned them in the first instance. For this reason,

---

SETTING A STRING

1 Set your scratchstock (essentially a scraping tool with a guiding edge) to the appropriate depth for the string.

2 If you are laying a new string, choose the correct width of scratchstock tool. Also, calculate the length of string required for the job.

3 Use the grinding edge to ensure that the groove is parallel to the edge of the job. Apply the adhesive with a dowel or off-cut.

4 Position the string in the groove and smooth it down with a hard, flat tool.

motifs of any sort should be respected. It is a truism that many motifs that have been perceived to be truly ugly have wound up in auction rooms, only to realise a great deal of cash.

As far as restoration is concerned, motifs should be treated in much the same way as any other inlay repair – but do adhere to the original design if possible.

METAL INLAYS

Metal inlays often spring out of their grooves because the wood surrounding them expands and they cannot. While repairs to these types of inlays can be attempted by the amateur restorer, it is a specialised process that is best left to experienced professionals.

> ### BUYING SPECIALIST TOOLS
> Although it is possible to make your own inlay tools – a scratchstock, for example – they can also be bought. Your best bet is to hunt around in the specialist press for adverts.

CUTTING A TEMPLATE AND LAYING A MOTIF

1 Cut out a paper template of the damaged area and use it to shape the veneer. Tape down the veneer before cutting it.

2 If you are cutting a new veneer, use a router to form the base. If you are restoring, clean with abrasive paper.

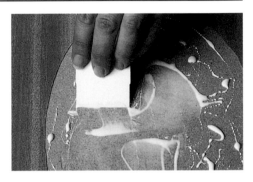

3 Paste adhesive onto the back of the new inlay. Use a sawtooth spreader to get even coverage and thus avoid awkward lumps.

4 Set the inlay in place, smooth it down and tape it securely.

5 Use a curved metal scraper to take off most of the excess veneer.

6 Remove the remaining excess with fine abrasive and then polish.

Preparing wooden surfaces for polish

Before wood can be polished, its surface must be prepared so that it is flat and smooth. In many ways, surface preparation is more important than the actual laying-on of the polish – if you do not get the surface completely smooth, any dents, scratches and other imperfections will be highlighted by the polish.

The amount of preparation required will depend on the condition of the piece of furniture and, in some cases, you may have to strip off paint or old varnish in order to get down to the wood surface. Proprietary paint-strippers make this chore simple.

STRIPPING VARNISH AND PAINT

Avoid taking an old piece of furniture to a firm which specialises in stripping. Such firms invariably dip entire pieces of furniture into caustic baths, a process which leaves the wood looking dead and lifeless. Stripping furniture yourself is time-consuming, but it is well worth the effort.

Chemical paint-strippers are readily available from hardware stores. Always treat them with respect: wear rubber gloves when handling them and use them only in a well-ventilated room. In addition to the stripper, you will need a scraper. For delicate or valuable furniture, do not use a steel scraper: it may gouge out chunks of wood. You would be better off using a homemade wooden scraper. To lay the stripper on, use an old, but clean, paintbrush. To clean paint out of awkward corners, try using a sharpened dowel. Steel wool and turpentine are useful for cleaning the grain after stripping.

Turned pieces and mouldings are best treated with stripping paste. This is spread thickly over the piece and can remove several layers of paint in one application. It is, however, expensive to use on large areas.

STRIPPING WAX AND POLISH

French polish can be removed with methyl alcohol and steel wool. The residue can be mopped up with paper towels.

Wax can usually be removed with turpentine and fine steel wool as you get down to the wood surface work with the grain.

STRIPPING VARNISH

1 Lay the workpiece on several layers of old newspaper and apply the chemical stripper with a paintbrush. Be sure to wear gloves.

2 Leave the stripper for 15 minutes or so to do its work. The varnish should start to blister and separate from the wood.

3 Scrape off the old finish and stripper with an improvised wooden tool. If necessary, apply further coats of stripper to get rid of all the old varnish.

4 Clean the grain of the stripped piece of wood with a pad of fine steel wool and neutralise the residue with methylated spirit.

ACHIEVING A GOOD FINISH

1 If the surface is rough, use a steel scraper to smooth it down. Always follow the grain of the wood.

2 Before applying a finish, smooth the surface down. Wrap abrasive paper around a square block so that you can apply an even pressure. Change to finer-grit abrasive paper as you progress.

3 Use a clean brush or cloth to apply stain. Again, follow the grain of the wood. Work the stain into the wood and leave it to dry. If necessary, apply several coats until you achieve the tone you want. Smooth down between coats and then put on a sealing finish of polish or varnish.

BLEACHING

Bare wood can be bleached or stained to alter its colour. Bleaching is not always predictable, but if you want to lighten the tone of a wood it can be quite successful, provided that the wood is relatively knot-free.

Use only diluted bleach and be sure to wear rubber gloves. Apply the bleach evenly with a clean paintbrush and allow it to settle in. When the wood has risen in colour, wash off the bleach with water. Bleaching will have the effect of raising the surface fibres of the wood. Smooth these down with fine abrasive paper before applying a finish.

STAINING

There are essentially two types of wood stain – one is water-based, the other is oil-based. Oil stains are more effective if you want a complete colour change; water stains are better if you want to emphasise the grain of the wood. Like bleach, water-based stains will raise the fibres of the wood, so wet the timber and sand it down before staining. Remember that you can only stain wood darker than it already is, not lighter.

Stains are usually applied with a clean brush. If you want to match the colour of a repair to a piece of furniture, be careful when wielding the brush as it is all too easy to stain the surrounding wood. Seal with an application of varnish or French polish. Some types tend to bleed.

USING A GOOSENECK SCRAPER

For cleaning certain mouldings and shaped pieces of wood a gooseneck scraper is invaluable. Made from flexible steel, the scraper can adapt to suit many profiles.

French polishing and waxing

A certain amount of mystique is attached to the technique of French polishing, and at its most professional level it is an art form in its own right. With a little practice a beginner will quickly be able to achieve surprisingly good results; patience and attention to detail are the most important skills required. No special tools are needed. The only essential is that it is carried out in warm, dry surroundings. However, bear in mind that the ingredients of French polish are highly flammable, so never use naked flames for heating or lighting.

The first stage in French polishing is called fadding or laying-on. Traditionally this is done with a fad or burnisher which is made from cotton sheet and lint-free cotton wool. The polish is applied in straight, even strokes following the direction of the grain, making sure that you do not stop in mid-stroke. Layers are built up until the desired depth is achieved. The polish should be allowed to dry for two to three hours and then sanded down with a fine, 250-grit silicon-carbide paper to remove any imperfections. Some people cheat a little at this stage and apply the first coats with a fine, squirrel-hair brush; this is just as good, but may require more sanding down between coats.

The purpose of this coat is to fill the open grain on the wood surface; for very deep-grained wood a grain-filler may have to be used before polishing.

For the burnishing stage, dilute the French polish 60-40 with methylated spirit and apply it with the fad in small, circular motions over the surface of the polish, again always travelling in the same direction as the grain. Some resistance or drag may be felt as the surface become tacky, but a small dab of boiled linseed oil applied to the bottom of the fad should cure this. The size of the circles should be gradually increased and then replaced with figure-of-eight movements before finally finishing with straight lines, as originally applied. If the polish becomes too thick you should stop and allow it to dry and then sand it back with the silicon-carbide paper before resuming polishing. A large surface may take several days of polishing to finish, but a rich, deep, burnished surface will be the result of your patience and labour. Any linseed oil left on the surface can be removed by loading your fad with methylated spirit and gently gliding it over the surface.

When you have achieved the desired depth of finish, you then simply allow it to dry for 24 hours and apply one or two layers of wax on top to protect it. If a non-shiny finish is required, the wax can be applied with a fine, 0000-grade wire wool.

WAXING

There are a huge variety of prepared furniture waxes to choose from; some are even scented! Generally speaking, it is best to opt for a type that contains beeswax. Always avoid polishes with a silicon content, which means that most aerosol-spray waxes, though easy to use, should be discarded.

Natural beeswax is not suitable for furniture polishing but a good, tinned beeswax will contain natural additives to help it harden and achieve a good shine. Some waxes are available with stains in them which help to colour wood or disguise damage to polished surfaces.

Wax can be applied to French-polished surfaces as described in the previous chapter or directly onto wood as a finish in its own right. It has been used as a finish since the Middle Ages, and most old furniture was originally polished in this way.

MAKING A BURNISHER OR FAD

  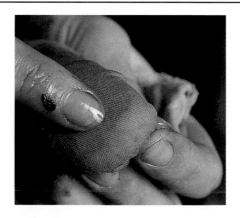

1 Use only lint-free, washed cotton for the burnisher. The filling can be made from a wad of ordinary cotton.

2 Fold the cotton cloth over the wadding to make a pear-shaped pad. Always add polish to the wadding and not to the face of the pad.

3 When you use the burnisher, you will find that the polish is forced from the wadding onto the cloth. Lubricate the burnisher sparingly with dabs of linseed oil.

FRENCH POLISHING

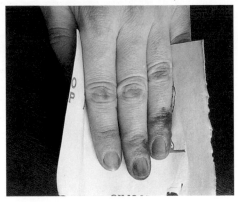

1 The first coat of French polish can be applied with a squirrel-hair brush. Always apply the polish in the same direction as the grain. Try to get an even coating so that all the pores in the wood are filled up.

2 When the first coat has dried, run over it with fine abrasive paper to remove any dust particles.

5 The finished work should have a deep sheen. Leave it for a few days and then apply a wax polish on top.

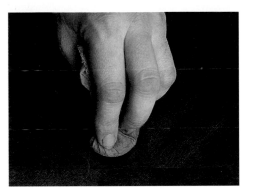

3 Apply subsequent coats of varnish using a homemade burnisher. Work in straight lines and as quickly as possible.

4 Build up layers of polish until you achieve the depth of colour you want. If your burnisher begins to stick, apply a few drops of linseed oil to the pad.

WAXING

It is a good idea to seal the wood with a layer of sanding sealer or French polish, which you can brush on first and then sand smooth when it has dried. This helps to protect the wood, as wax takes a long time to harden and provide a protective coat.

The wax can then be applied with a soft cloth, an even coating being applied and allowed to harden before burnishing with a separate, clean, soft cloth. It is important that each coat be allowed to dry completely, as any subsequent coats will simply remove the previous coats and a poor, patchy finish will be the result.

To apply wax in awkward mouldings or turnings, a 1in (2.5cm), soft paintbrush, with the hairs trimmed down to a ¾in (1.9cm) stubble, is an excellent tool, which will stay soft wrapped in a white-spirit-dampened cloth and stored in a glass jar or plastic bag.

1 The first coating of wax can be applied with a wad of fine (0000-gauge) steel wool. Work the wax gently into the grain.

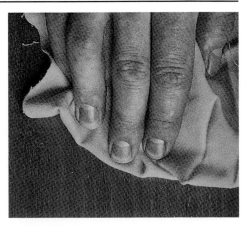

2 When the wax has hardened, polish it with a clean, dry cloth. Apply additional coats as required, allowing each layer to dry before applying the next. Some surfaces may need several coats.

Varnishing and burnishing

Varnishing has the unfortunate reputation of being a poor man's version of polishing. Although varnish is easier to apply and is tougher, it lacks the finesse of polish. However, for certain practical pieces of furniture – chairs are a classic example – it has no equal.

Choose your varnish carefully. Today most varnishes are polyurethanes; they are hard-wearing and, if applied with care, last for a very long time. However, polyurethane varnishes often contain pigment, and this can discolour wood, especially if the varnish is applied in several layers. Clear varnishes are available, but they are more expensive.

Most varnishes give a gloss finish (although you can obtain satin-finish varnishes). This is a point worth considering before you decide to use varnish – gloss is fine for many objects, but in some instances it can detract from the appearance of the wood.

Although they can be sprayed, varnishes are usually brushed on. Because of the consistency of varnish, brushing often leaves 'streaks', which can impair the appearance of the finish. For this reason, it is usual to burnish a piece of furniture after it has been varnished to get rid of unwanted marks.

TOOLS AND MATERIALS

- clean, good-quality paintbrush
- 150-grit abrasive paper
- 400-grit wet-and-dry paper
- sanding block
- good-quality varnish
- burnishing cream
- turpentine

LAYING ON VARNISH

Before varnishing a piece of furniture, make sure it is completely clean and dust-free, especially at the corners. If possible, apply the varnish in a dust-free room – dust is the ultimate bane of all varnishing procedures.

Brush on the first coat (thinned 50:50 with turpentine), following the direction of the grain. When the coat is dry, after 24 hours or so rub over it with abrasive paper to remove dust and 'nibs'. Wipe off the dust created by

VARNISHING

1 The surface must be completely dust-free before brushing on the first coat.

2 When applying varnish, always follow the grain of the wood.

3 Sand down between coats - this will guarantee a good finish.

4 Apply subsequent coats with a clean brush, trying to avoid 'build-ups' in corners.

BURNISHING

1 *Allow the varnish to harden before rubbing it down with fine wet-and-dry paper. It is best to wrap wet-and-dry paper around a sanding block.*

2 *Check the surface against the light and continue sanding if necessary.*

3 *Work burnishing cream into the surface of the varnish with a soft cloth.*

4 *Polish off the residue with a clean cloth to achieve a high gloss.*

sanding and apply a second coat of varnish – this time unthinned. Keep adding layers of varnish – three should do – until you achieve the finish you desire. Do not forget to sand down between applications.

BURNISHING

When your final coat of varnish has completely dried out — it is best to play safe and leave it for three days – you can start burnishing the surface to a high-gloss finish.

Start by removing the worst of the 'nibs' and dust marks with a sheet of 400-grit wet-and-dry paper wrapped around a sanding block or a square off-cut of wood. Lubricate the wet-and-dry paper with liberal amounts of water as you work (varnish is impervious to water, so the wood cannot get damaged).

Wipe off the residue left by the wet-and-dry paper, using a dry cloth. Position the work-piece against the light to see if there are any ripples or blemishes that could be removed by more sanding.

To restore the shine to the surface, rub on burnishing cream, which is a very fine abrasive. Do this with a soft cloth and work in straight lines if possible. Polish off after burnishing using a clean cloth.

TAKING CARE OF PAINTBRUSHES

There are several things you can do to extend the life of a paintbrush:

● after using a brush to apply a solvent-based material like varnish, wash it out thoroughly with turpentine

● after cleaning the brush with turpentine, wash it in soapy water to get rid of any oily residues

● wrap a rubber band around the end of the brush before storing it; this holds the strands together so that they do not splay apart

● never stand brushes in jars, as this turns the strands: the best way to store them is to hang them up vertically; failing this, keep them flat

● if you want to store a brush temporarily and do not want to go to the bother of cleaning it thoroughly, suspend it in a jar of water (many brushes have holes through their handles for this purpose). Simply slide a stout wire through the hole and hang the brush into a container of water

Painting wood

Paint, contrary to traditional belief, can make furniture more attractive. But to look effective it has to be well applied. There are several ways of applying paint. The most obvious of these is with a brush, but the brush can be handled in many different ways to achieve a multitude of effects. If you are restoring a valued antique, you would be best not to paint it, but if you have a run-of-the-mill piece which you want to make interesting, try adding paint.

PAINTING WITH A BRUSH

Furniture does not have to be stripped before being painted, but the surface must be clean, dry and smooth. Use wet-and-dry paper to eliminate lumps and bumps from a previously painted piece. This will also provide a key for the subsequent layer of paint. If necessary, you can fill dents with a proprietary wood-filler before painting.

If you are painting bare wood, you will need a primer coat, an undercoat and a topcoat; the primer seals the wood and the undercoat prepares for the finish. Primers are universal, but undercoats are usually matched to a selection of topcoats. When you buy your paints, make sure you get compatible types.

Choose your brushes carefully – poor-quality ones tend to lose their bristles into the paint as you apply it.

MIXING PAINTS

If you want to blend two colours together to achieve a specific hue it is not always easy to get an even mix. Here are some hints.

● Use a paint kettle as your mixing bowl, otherwise you will end up in a mess. Pour the tinting paint into the body colour and make a note of the quantities of each paint.

● When you mix the two paints together, use a clean, straight length of doweling. As you swirl the two paints together, draw the stick upwards. This will ensure that the paint mixes evenly.

● If you have large quantities of paint to mix, consider buying a special paint-mixer. These gadgets fit onto ordinary electric drills and can simplify the chore.

PAINTING A DOOR

1 *Dip the brush in paint up to half the bristle length and then use a piece of wire or string across the kettle to scrape off the excess.*

2 *Where necessary, as with doors, apply paint to intricate areas, such as mouldings, before painting in the panels.*

3 *Fill in the other areas by painting first with, and then across, the wood grain, to give an even paint layer.*

4 *Finally, finish off the area with light brush strokes following the grain of the wood.*

KEEPING RECORDS

A good tip to observe is to keep records of the quantities of colours that you mix to create colours and effects. This way you will have a record to refer to should you wish to recreate them in the future.

MARBLING

To 'marble' paint you need a stiff-haired brush, a firm feather and several small, natural sponges or, alternatively, sheets of crumpled paper. To achieve a good marbling effect, you must have a sound groundwork. Over this, brush a thin topcoat. The graining pattern is arrived at by dragging, swirling or dabbing a combination of implements over the wet undercoat. For interesting effects, try dipping the implements in dark paint.

GRAINING

Wood-grain effects can be achieved using a stiff feather or a good-quality, fine, artist's paintbrush. Wood-graining is usually done on a dry undercoat, although techniques differ. If you wish to try your hand at wood-graining, first study real wood grain – it is easy to get carried away with a paintbrush and produce something that is totally unlike a genuine wood grain.

HIGHLIGHTING

Once you have painted a piece of furniture, you may think that it requires a bit of finesse or finishing off. One way of achieving this is to highlight edges and corners. Always use masking tape to define your lines.

Laying down masking tape in parallel lines takes some practice, so think twice before tackling awkward shapes. If you do lay down masking tape, make sure that it is firmly stuck down. Having painted your highlight lines with a narrow brush, pull off the tape while the paint is still wet, otherwise you run the risk of ripping off dry paint which has adhered to both surfaces.

Top
Marbling is an interesting paint effect that can be achieved by laying wet paint on a wet base coat, using feathers, sponges or paintbrushes.
Above
Highlights are best laid down using masking tape. If you want to highlight mouldings, a steady hand and a fine brush are called for.
Right
A classic example of graining, achieved by delicately brushing onto dry paint.

Stencilling and spray-painting

Stencilling and spray-painting are two techniques that are often used together. If you want a coloured motif on a piece of furniture, your best plan is to use a stencil in combination with a spray gun, airbrush or aerosol.

STENCILLING

A stencil is essentially a paper or card cut-out that can be sprayed or painted through or around to create an image. A good stencil can be used many times to create a multiplicity of identical images. Stencils can be cut from many materials and the choice of material largely depends on how many times the image is to be reproduced. A paper stencil, for example, will take just one spraying; a card stencil will take several sprayings; and a waxed-card stencil will take many sprayings. Plastic stencils, which last virtually forever, are difficult to make yourself, but you can buy them – although this means, of course, that you are constrained by the manufacturer's choice of designs.

USING AEROSOLS

If you want to reproduce an image several times over, the easiest way is to spray using a stencil. Even if you are the most meticulous and thorough of persons, there can be no denying that spraying is not only more efficient but also more effective than brushing. This is largely because it ensures a more even coverage.

If you decide to spray paint, you have the option of using an aerosol can or a spray gun.

Aerosols have several advantages. They are easy to use, relatively cheap to buy and clean. Their drawbacks are that they come in a limited range of colours and finishes and they are not always compatible with underlay paints. When using aerosols, be sure to have adequate ventilation – they are highly toxic and the effects of their vapour can be overwhelming.

USING SPRAY EQUIPMENT

If you have a complete piece of furniture that you want to paint it may be worth your while to hire a spray gun. Spray guns, in the hands of an expert, give even coverage, but they are not always easy to handle.

If you want to use a spray gun, you will need also an air-compressor – the two are usually hired or sold together. Before you hire or buy a spray gun, check that it will handle the type of paint you want to use. If you wish to use cellulose paint, be warned: these paints are highly noxious and can be fatal if used in confined spaces.

If you want to do fine, decorative work, consider buying an airbrush. Airbrushes, particularly the more basic types, can be surprisingly inexpensive to buy (you will be unlikely to find anyone willing to hire out an airbrush). If you do decide on an airbrush, check that it can take the types of paint that you wish to use and be sure to invest in an air supply (either pressurised air cans or a mini air-compressor).

Whatever type of spray equipment you decide on, and whichever type of medium you use, be sure to allow adequate ventilation. All spray equipment produces fumes of one sort or another.

Left
A classic example of creative stencilling. Several different motifs were cut out of card and sprayed through to create sound and cohesive images.

STENCILLING TIPS
Successful stencilling demands forethought, draughtsmanship, a calm hand and a cool mind – a single slip can ruin a design. Draw out your design on paper and transfer it to the stencil card. Cut out the card with a scalpel or sharp handyman's knife. Patch up any nicks in the card with masking tape before spraying onto it.

USING AEROSOLS

1 Prepare your design carefully, then mask off the areas that you do not wish to be sprayed.

2 Having masked off the area with a combination of paper and tape, start to spray.

3 Before the aerosol paint dries (which is rapidly), peel off the masking tape.

4 Pull off each strip of masking tape sharply so that it does not disrupt the paint layer.

SAFETY – AEROSOLS AND SPRAY GUNS

All aerosols produce noxious fumes. They are not always noticed at first, but they can induce severe headaches, if not worse. Similarly, spray guns and airbrushes emit particles of paint into the immediate atmosphere. If you use an aerosol, spray gun or airbrush, allow yourself plenty of fresh air. In other words, keep an extractor fan going, open a window or spray only in an extremely large room. If you plan to use any sort of spray equipment for any length of time (say, 20 minutes), hire (or buy) eye goggles and a face mask.

Construction types

New timbers from South America and west Africa, combined with new techniques and the appearance of sophisticated tools, have dramatically changed furniture construction. Whereas, in the old days, there was 'only one way to make furniture', there are now hundreds of ways to construct the bits and pieces that litter the average living-room.

Early furniture was heavy and clumsy, mainly because it was constructed from hand-hewn boards and the sawyers had little consideration for the quality of the timber. As tools improved and skills advanced, furniture-making became sophisticated; it became the province of the cabinetmaker and no longer that of the carpenter, whereas the carpenter built houses, the cabinetmaker made furniture. Somewhere along the line, art and design became embroiled with furniture-making and the whole concept changed.

TRADITIONAL METHODS

In the old days, adhesives were not very strong, so the more astute cabinetmakers devised joints that would remain stable over a long period of time, regardless of the glue used. Their ideal was to make pieces of furniture that would stay whole forever. They used glue to hold pieces together temporarily, trusting that their jointing methods would be strong enough to hold the pieces of wood securely. Of course, they did not understand the effects of the climate on furniture; however, by and large, the old methods are still the best. New and cheaper jointing methods have appeared over the past few decades, but only time will tell if they will last.

Glues and adhesives have obviously improved in strength as a result of modern research, but few glues can surpass the strength of a well-made joint.

Below left
This sewing table was constructed comparatively recently, using traditional jointing methods. The construction method took into account the use of the table, which demanded sound joints to sustain the constant vibration of the machine.

Below
Although the joints in this chest are strong, their strength largely depends on the quality of the glue used to make them.

MODERN METHODS

Modern jointing methods invariably rely on the strength of the adhesive. If they do not, they rely on screws or nails.

There can be no denying that modern adhesives are immensely strong. But they are not necessarily strong in all situations. For example, some modern joints held together with PVA adhesive may appear sound, but in damp conditions they begin to disintegrate. Even the seemingly indestructible epoxy adhesives succumb, quite readily, to the pressure of expanding wood.

Manmade materials like chipboard and plywood have some advantage over natural wood in that they are less likely to warp and bend. Consequently, it is cheaper to joint such materials using modern methods; i.e., using adhesives and screws. Indeed, many modern pieces of furniture, like kitchen cabinets, are best made out of chipboard or MDF.

Below and right.
This Art Deco-style sideboard was constructed from manmade boards using modern jointing methods.

Construction methods

1 *Joint cut from the middle of the piece*
2 *A dovetail halving*
3 *Joint cut into the thickness of the piece*
4 *Joint cut into the end of the piece*

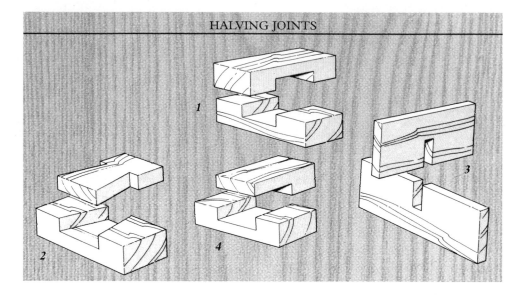

HALVING JOINTS

TRADITIONAL METHODS

The cabinetmaker of old gained his reputation from making sound joints – his very livelihood depended on it. Certain joints have become familiar, such as the mortise and tenon, the dovetail and the laplock (or 'halving joint', as it is now called).

None of these joints are easy, and some are exceptionally difficult, to make successfully. It is little wonder that old furniture that has been well made is so revered.

NEW METHODS

The mass-production of furniture, combined with new types of wood and materials, has inevitably led to the appearance of new jointing methods.

MORTISE-AND-TENON JOINTS

1 *Pegging*
2 *Wedging*
3 *Doubling the tenon*
4 *Angling the tenon*
5 *Halving the tenon*
6 *Mitring tenons*

PANEL JOINTS

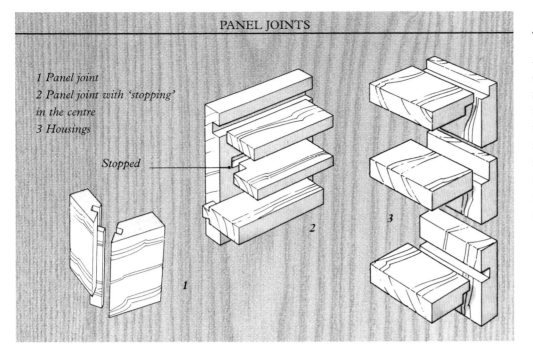

1 Panel joint
2 Panel joint with 'stopping' in the centre
3 Housings

Stopped

2

3

1

KNOCK-DOWN FITTINGS

Manmade boards like chipboard and plywood cannot be successfully jointed using traditional methods – the structure of the boards is such that they cannot take the stress imparted on them. It is hardly surprising, therefore, that new fixing methods specifically devised for manmade boards have been produced. These are usually called 'knock-down' fittings, simply because they are easy to assemble and easy to 'knock down'.

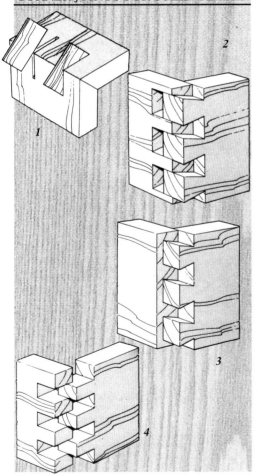

1
2
3
4
5
6

Boards

1 Plywood
2 Multi-ply
3 Blockboard
4 Hardboard
5 Medium-density-fibre board
6 Chipboard

CORNER JOINTS FOR SOLID TIMBER

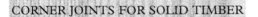

2

1

3

4

1 Keyed mitre
2 Through dovetail
3 Lap dovetail
4 Comb joint

BRIDLE JOINTS

Basic bridle joint

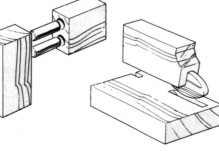

1 Dowels
2 Biscuits

Dismantling tables and chairs

Dismantling furniture is not a matter to be taken lightly. There is one golden rule which applies to both beginner and expert: do not dismantle a piece of valued furniture unless it is absolutely necessary. If you are left with no choice, because the piece you are dealing with is a shambles, but you see some future in it, examine it carefully before you start work. Above all, look out for nails and screws. These are often carefully hidden and disguised behind layers of varnish or polish – if you start dismantling and have overlooked a nail fixing the workpiece may end up ruined beyond all redemption.

DISMANTLING A TABLE

In many ways, dismantling a table is the most difficult of any task. This is largely because the bits and pieces are large and therefore cumbersome to handle.

Before you start, label each piece with sticky tape, noting that 'Piece A' joints onto 'Piece B', etc. If you do not carry out this basic procedure you will find yourself in chaos at the end of the day.

Once you have removed all the fixing devices, such as the nails and the screws, you may find that it is not easy to prise the various sections apart. Some pieces may be 'fox-wedged', meaning that they were intended never to be taken apart. In such cases, you will have little option but to use a fine saw.

Try knocking the joints apart with a rubber mallet before you resort to more vicious tactics. Before hitting the piece of furniture with a mallet protect the vulnerable wood with an off-cut of soft wood.

DISMANTLING A CHAIR

Taking apart a chair is much like dismantling a table. One of the gentlest ways of separating pieces is to use a sash clamp in reverse; in other words, put the butts outwards and turn the lever to push apart. If you use a sash clamp in this way you may find that you have enough scope to insert the necessary blobs of glue to cure the defect. If you really want to go ahead and separate all the pieces, be sure to label them.

When separating pieces of furniture, the important thing to remember is the piece itself. It is all too easy to get carried away and strike a piece too hard. Always respect old furniture and how it was put together. If you are tackling an old piece, bear in mind that it may have been constructed traditionally. In other words, modern dismantling methods may not be totally suitable.

DISMANTLING A TABLE

1 Before dismantling a table or any other piece of furniture, label all the corresponding parts.

2 Carefully remove all visible nails and screws before you start dismembering the joints of the workpiece.

3 You may have to resort to the use of a mallet in order to separate pieces. If so, protect the piece from heavy blows by using an off-cut.

DISMANTLING A CHAIR

1 *Rickety chairs are invariably weak at the front. Remove blocks so that the joints themselves can be approached.*

2 *Most loose joints will pull apart with a straight tug. If need be, place the chair on a bench and look for nails and screws.*

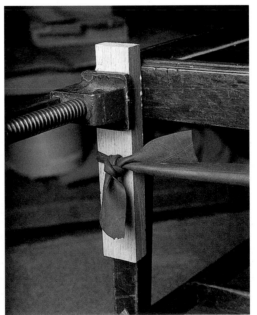

3 *Once you have separated a joint, clean up the parts. In this photograph the dowels of a joint are being scraped with a chisel.*

4 *Once all the pieces have been freed from residue, glue and dirt they can be reglued and clamped together.*

USING SOLVENTS

Some glues (or 'adhesives', as they are more correctly called) respond to solvents. In other words, if you apply an appropriate solvent, the glue may dissolve or melt, making it easier to separate a joint.

Traditional glues are invariably animal-based, and so are soluble in water. If you stumble across an old joint that will not come apart, try applying water. If this does not work, try the steam from a kettle. Be sure not to wound the wood or melt the surrounding finish.

Modern glues are trickier than their traditional counterparts. Many change their initial character after they have set. However, acetone, turpentine and methyl alcohol are all worth trying if you want to soften a stubborn adhesive.

Dismantling cabinet furniture

Dismantling a piece of cabinet furniture – e.g., a chest of drawers – is altogether different from tackling any other type of furniture. It is in cabinet (box-like) furniture that the craftsman shows his or her art. In cabinet furniture, be it a box, a desk or a chest of drawers, the joints are all-important.

Dovetail joints are found in most drawer fronts and sometimes in adjoining tops. For a very good reason – they are difficult to make satisfactorily – dovetail joints are revered by novices. There can be no doubt that a good dovetail joint is immensely strong and consequently there is seldom any need to take one apart. However, the other joints in a cabinet are vulnerable and do occasionally need to

be taken apart. The moral when dismantling a cabinet is: do not do it until you have to, and, when you do, to look out for hidden and secret joints

DISMANTLING A DRAWER

If you do have to take a drawer apart – perhaps it has become unsteady – the first thing to do is to take stock of the joints.

You will most likely find dovetail joints holding the sides to the front. Old dovetails – those with narrow tails – should be steamed with water to loosen the glue before dismantling. New dovetails – those that are evenly spaced and comparatively wide – may prove easier to dislodge since they were most likely

machine-made and the fittings were therefore not so tight.

When dismantling a drawer, be gentle. Use an off-cut of timber to protect any wood that you hit with your wooden mallet – doing this will spread the weight of the blows and will consequently prevent bruising (use a rubber mallet if you are at all unsure). And, obviously, be sure to remove any nails or pins which may superficially hold the structure together.

Dismantling a chest of drawers
Learn how it was put together before you take it apart!

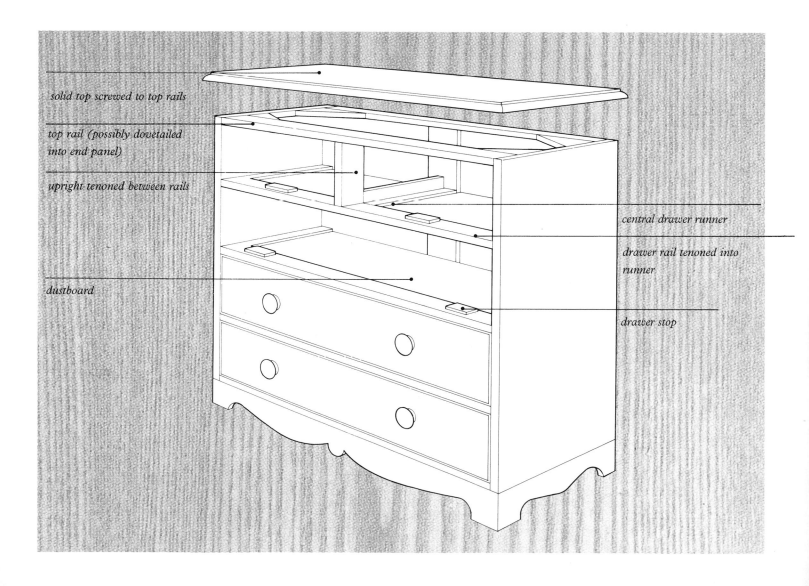

solid top screwed to top rails

top rail (possibly dovetailed into end panel)

upright tenoned between rails

dustboard

central drawer runner

drawer rail tenoned into runner

drawer stop

DISMANTLING A DRAWER

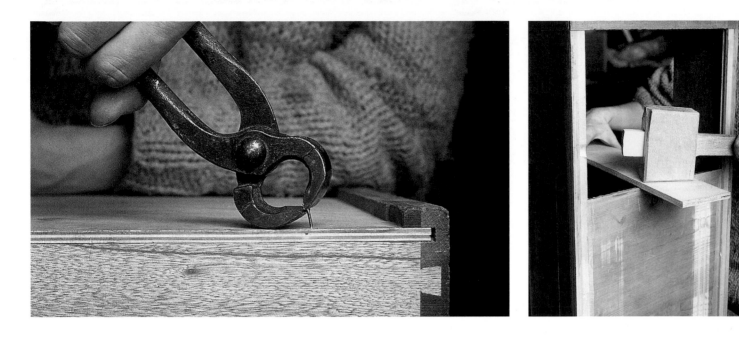

1 Start dismantling a drawer by removing any panel pins that hold the base in place.

2 Having removed the pins, knock the base out of its grooves using a wooden mallet.

3 With the base out of the way, tap out the face, using a mallet and a protective pad of wood or cloth.

4 Old dovetail joints in drawers are smaller than more recent, mechanically cut joints.

Gluing and clamping

Perhaps surprisingly, there is something of an art to gluing and clamping, especially when more than two parts are involved. The purpose of clamping is to force pieces together so that the glue between them makes a genuine bond. It is wrong to assume that glue will automatically join two pieces together satisfactorily. For gluing to be effective any two pieces that are to be joined together have to be in intimate contact. Clamping consolidates this bond and ensures that it is readily made. Clamping is very necessary in woodwork because it encourages bonding between materials.

METHODS OF CLAMPING
The G-clamp is the most universally used clamp. It comes in a variety of sizes and can, using a variety of methods, be adapted to suit many situations. G-clamps are often worked in pairs to ensure that the weight is distributed evenly; to even the balance between two G-clamps place a batten between the two opposing jaws.

Sash clamps have a more specialised purpose, but they are extremely useful to the furniture-restorer. Sash clamps can bridge comparatively wide gaps, which is useful if you are rejoining something like a chair or a table.

Tourniquet clamps are useful if you want to clasp an entire workpiece together, because they provide equal pressure on all joints. You can improvise your own tourniquet clamp from nylon, or you can buy specially made versions which include a clamping device.

REASSEMBLING A TABLETOP
When joining boards together to reassemble a tabletop, use sash clamps to effect the join.

DEALING WITH GLUE STAINS
If you are clamping pieces of furniture together, it stands to reason that a certain amount of glue will ooze out. Excess glue can stain fabrics and wood and should be dealt with as soon as possible.

Water-based adhesives, like animal glue and PVA, should be mopped up as soon as the clamps are tightened. Use a damp rag to clean off residues.

Oil-based adhesives must be tackled using a suitable solvent as soon as they appear. Most oil-based adhesives respond to turpentine, so wipe up with a turpentine-dampened rag.

It is best to use at least three clamps so that they can be placed alternately on either side of the board. If you do not position the clamps alternately, the top may be pulled into a V-shape.

REASSEMBLING MITRES
Mitred corners should be clamped with special, right-angled clamps. There are many varieties of these clamps and you should consider hiring one if you have only a limited amount of work to do.

REASSEMBLING MOULDINGS
Small mouldings that are to be glued together can be held in place perfectly satisfactorily with masking or any other sort of adhesive tape. Alternatively, you can knock in small panel pins and pull them out again once the adhesive has dried.

REASSEMBLING A CHAIR
Few chairs are square on all their corners, and the back is usually narrower than the front. So if you were to use a sash clamp, the structure would be pulled out of true. In addition, the heads of sash clamps would most likely damage the surface of the wood. If you want to clamp a chair together, either use webbing clamps or build up your own method, using a combination of clamps.

Left
If you are clamping several boards or a frame together, anchor them to a sound base using G-clamps. Then apply sash clamps to pull the sections into a whole.

Top
Reassembling a chair is no easy task. Make your own tourniquet clamps where sash or G-clamps cannot be applied.

Above
Use sash clamps carefully and do not get carried away when twisting the arm. If you are rejoining tabletop panels, alternate the clamps above and below the boards.

Far left
To prevent bruising of wood surfaces, always use off-cuts of timber between the work and the jaws of the clamps.

GLUING JOINTS
Always do a dry run before applying glue. It may set before you realise the complexity of clamping a joint and then you will be in trouble!

Repairs to panels

Panels in old furniture are invariably made up from a series of boards joined together. In tabletops and the large, flat components of articles of cabinet furniture, such as sideboards and dressers, the boards are usually thick enough to allow for a joint of some kind. Feathered joints and tongue-and-groove joints are the ones most commonly used. A feather is a thin strip of wood that fits into grooves cut into the edges of the boards.

Thin panels, such as those found in cabinet doors and the bottoms of drawers, are usually rebated or just butted and glued together.

Panels of all kinds are particularly vulnerable to climatic changes. They are likely to warp or even split. Central-heating systems are especially bad for furniture.

A split along a joint in a panel should be comparatively easy to repair, but of course you will have to remove the panel from its frame. Some panels are held in place by strips of beading. Lever off the beading in order to remove the panel. Having removed the panel, clean up the joint, insert more glue and then clamp the assembly together. Sash clamps are often the best option, but be sure to protect the wood from the jaws. The easiest way of doing this is to insert off-cuts.

If a split does not run along a joint, the remedy is not quite so simple. You will have to insert a dowel to strengthen the join.

MAKING DOWEL INSERTS

If you want to use a dowel in the repair of a split panel, you will be unlikely to find ready-made doweling that matches the wood. Do not despair! Making your own dowels is straightforward. Of course, you will have to obtain a piece of wood that matches the colour and quality of the panel, but this should not prove too difficult, as many suppliers have off-cuts of exotic timber.

1 Drill a hole of the appropriate diameter through a stout piece of metal. Then hammer your sliver of wood through the hole. This seemingly crude method in fact produces perfectly rounded dowels.

2 Scribe two lines down the side of the dowel using the pin on a marking gauge. These grooves will allow excess adhesive to escape when you use the dowel in the repair.

REPAIRING A CRACKED EDGE

1 Cracks are quite common in thick panels. Here, the edge of an oak table has split.

2 Make your own dowel insert from a piece of matching wood. Mark off the length of the dowel on the drill bit and wrap a piece of masking tape around it.

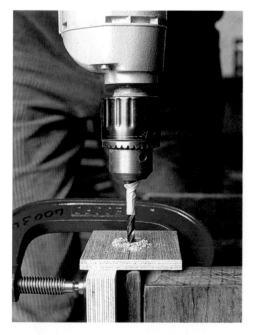

3 Drill into the edge of the panel through a protective off-cut of wood – the hole should go straight down the middle of the crack. Use the tape on the drill bit as a depth guide.

4 Smear PVA adhesive over the dowel before tapping it into the hole. Excess adhesive should ooze out via the grooves in the dowel.

5 When the adhesive has set, level the end of the dowel flush with the edge of the panel, using a sharp chisel.

Repairs to chipboard

Chipboard is not a particularly strong material and consequently it can suffer severely from superficial damage. Because it is so easy to scratch, dent and break, chipboard is often covered with a veneer or laminate of some kind, which also serves the purpose of adding a decorative skin to the chipboard. Plastic laminates are tough and are usually stuck to the surface with contact adhesive. If a laminate lifts from the surface of the chipboard, it can usually be stuck back down again, provided that both surfaces are dry and clean. Melamine

is a common facing for chipboard.

Melamine is paper impregnated with a synthetic resin and is not very durable. If a sheet of melamine-faced chipboard gets severely damaged it is often cheaper and quicker to replace it with a new sheet.

Repairs to chipboard are difficult and rarely invisible; large areas of damage are best resolved with the complete replacement of the damaged areas.

SUPERFICIAL REPAIRS TO A CHIPBOARD SHEET

The easiest way to repair a dent or hole in a sheet of chipboard is to use a filler. Use a two-part epoxy filler, which is both strong and durable. Clean up the dent or hole as much as possible and make sure that it is dry and free from grease. Mix up the filler according to the manufacturer's instructions. Use a flexible filling knife to spread the filler over the hole. Act quickly, as once the two parts are mixed together the filler will begin to solidify. Leave the filler slightly proud of the surface of the board and allow it to harden - this should take only 15 minutes or so. When the filler

has set, sand it down flush with the surface of the board. If you want to colour the filler, which is usually dull and grey, use an oil paint finely applied with a good-quality paintbrush. Coloured fillers are also available, although an exact match is unlikely. You may have to apply several coats of paint to disguise the repair completely.

REPAIRING A BROKEN CORNER

The corners of chipboard tabletops are particularly vulnerable to knocks, and whole pieces can quite easily be broken off. One way of disguising a broken corner is to round it off using a rasp. Of course, to make the disguise effective you will also have to round off the other three corners of the tabletop.

If the damage is too severe for this treatment, a new cornerpiece can be fitted, but this is not likely to be very strong. If you do fit a new piece, resurface the entire table with a sheet of laminate. Use contact adhesive to stick the sheet of laminate to the surface of the chipboard.

REPAIRING A DAMAGED EDGE

When the edge of a chipboard panel is damaged, it may appear to split into layers. This means that the edges of the damaged area will be thicker than the rest of the panel. The broken piece cannot simply be stuck back in place because that would mean that there would be a bump on both faces. To make a decent repair, the chipboard must be cut back to beyond the damaged area. The easiest way of cutting out a section of chipboard is to use an electric jigsaw; failing that, use a tenon saw. Make sure the cuts are square. Use the cut-out as a template for measuring out the insert and, when you start sawing, make allowances for the thickness of the blade.

DISGUISING A REPAIR WITH A PATTERN

If the centre of a laminated sheet of chipboard is damaged, you may have to cut out the damaged section of laminate and insert a new piece. You may find that laminate of that colour is no longer on sale. If so, insert a geometrical shape in a contrasting colour to make up a pattern.

SUPERFICIAL REPAIRS USING EPOXY FILLER

1 Mix up the two parts of the filler on an off-cut. Mix the filler in the quantities recommended by the manufacturer.

2 Spread the filler over the damaged area, using a flexible knife. When the filler is hard, sand it smooth and tint it with paint.

TOUCHING UP SCRATCHES

Scratches on veneered chipboard can often be hidden by applying wax polish. If this fails, try rubbing a stick of pure beeswax over the area; this will fill the scratches and render them barely visible.

REPAIRING A BROKEN EDGE

1 *The edges of chipboard are notoriously vulnerable. The best remedy for a damaged edge is to cut out the damaged area and insert a new piece.*

2 *Mark out the piece you want to remove and drill access holes at the corners. Cut out the section with a tenon saw or an electric jigsaw.*

3 *Cut a new section to fit and glue it in place with PVA adhesive. To match up the surfaces, lay a flat block of wood over the repair and tap sharply with a hammer.*

4 *When the adhesive has set, chamfer the edges of the repair with a plane. To complete the repair, either lay on a sheet of laminate or stain the insert.*

Repairing broken chair legs

Of all articles of furniture, chairs suffer from the most abuse. It is hardly surprising, therefore, that they are often in need of repairing. Back legs of chairs often break at the point where the seat rails join them. Luckily, such breaks are quite simple to repair. However, if the seat rails break, the chair may have to be dismantled, the damaged section cut out and a new piece spliced in. This is tricky and requires some skill, as new joints may have to be cut.

REPAIRS TO BACK LEGS

Most breaks in back legs occur because the chair has been tilted backwards by its occupant. This places an undue strain on the wood, which invariably splits along the grain. These breaks are comparatively easy to repair because the pieces can simply be glued back together again.

The type of adhesive you use is all-important. PVA adhesive is probably your best option, as it is both strong and cheap. However, if the chair is to be sited in a damp room – such as a bathroom or kitchen – consider using a waterproof adhesive instead.

Much of the skill involved in repairing a broken leg lies in the clamping – sometimes special blocks have to be made to ensure an even pressure all round. It is important to clamp from the sides, as well as front to back, so that the joints stay in alignment. Always go through a dry run of the assembly first to avoid messy problems later.

REPAIRS TO FRONT LEGS

Front legs of chairs usually break immediately below the seat-rail joint. Such breaks can be repaired using a sturdy dowel, but this may mean dismantling the chair to some extent. If you have to insert a dowel to link the two broken pieces together, the hardest part of the job is aligning the holes; you will probably have to make a special jig.

REPAIRING A SPLIT BACK LEG

1 Splits follow the grain of the wood and so are comparatively easy to repair.

2 Cut a shallow wedge from an off-cut of wood and insert it into the spilt to open it up.

REPAIRING A WOBBLY JOINT

1 Dismantle the joint and scrape off old glue with a sharp chisel.

2 Cut down the length of tenon. This is a tricky operation, so take your time.

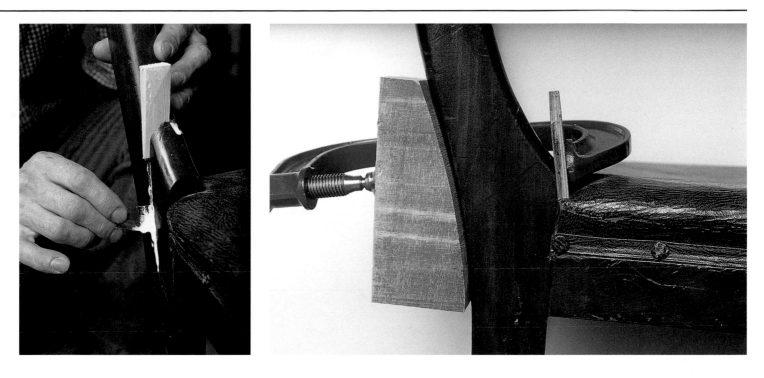

3 Using a knife blade or a fine piece of plastic, smear PVA adhesive into the split.

4 Wipe off excess adhesive with a damp rag and clamp the pieces together. If necessary, shape a block of wood to the profile of the leg so that the pressure is spread evenly.

3 Cut a fine wedge from a suitable off-cut.

4 Smear PVA adhesive over the wedge and force it into the cut in the tenon.

5 Reassemble the joint after spreading glue over the mating parts

Restoring corners/ frame repairs

Frames serve a very practical role in furniture, as they hold panels in place. They usually have strong mortise-and-tenon joints to hold them together. The joints have to be strong in order to take the strain if the wood warps. However, in old pieces of furniture, these joints sometimes separate because they can no longer withstand the pressure. Repairing frame joints is quite simple in theory but, in practice, the clamping can be difficult.

It is also quite common for the tenon in a frame joint to break, especially if the frame receives a certain amount of wear and tear. If the tenon snaps, you will have little option but to fit a false one.

Corners on chairs, tables and chests are very vulnerable to knocks and grazes. Repairing a broken or damaged corner on an old piece of furniture is a difficult task, and represents one of the areas where the restorer's skill has to match the cabinetmaker's. To effect a decent repair to a corner, you will have to buy a wood which matches the piece of furniture. When you buy the wood, make sure that it is seasoned, and obviously do your best to match colour and quality.

Be sure that your tools are clean and sharp before tackling a job like patching a corner – blunt tools are a hindrance.

1 Plane down the damaged corner so that you end up with two flat faces.

REPAIRING A BROKEN FRAME

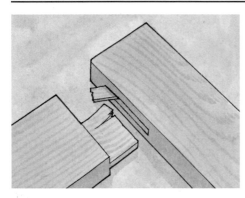

1 A broken tenon is a common reason for a frame failing.

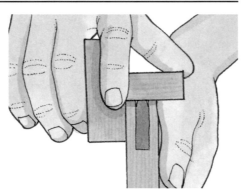

2 Before cutting a false tenon, measure the width of the mortise.

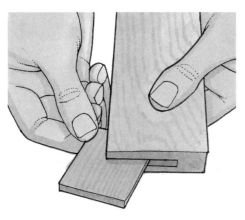

3 Cut a slot in the end of the rail, making sure that the slot is on the lower or inner side of any join to help to disguise it. Glue in a matching piece of wood to create a false tenon.

4 Reassemble the joint, using PVA adhesive. Clamp the joint until it sets.

3 Lay a matching section of wood over the repair and mark around it.

REPAIRING A DAMAGED CORNER

2 *Check that the planed faces are perfectly flat and even.*

4 *Plane an edge of the new section flat and stick it in place.*

5 *When the glue has set, cut off the excess wood with a tenon saw.*

REPAIRING A DAMAGED CORNER (Continued)

6 *Using a chisel, shape the section to match the profile of the furniture.*

7 *Scribe a cutting line on the new piece to outline the corner.*

8 *Having shaped the first piece, align a second and mark it to fit.*

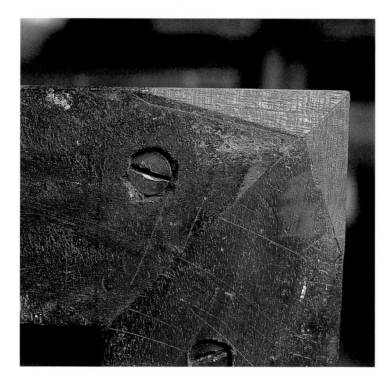

9 *Shape and fix the second insert in place so that the two form a right-angled corner.*

10 *When the glue has set, smooth the repair using fine abrasive paper.*

12 The fully restored piece of furniture
with the corner repair hardly visible.

11 Apply polish to the repair so that it
matches the colour of the piece
of furniture.

Drawer repairs

Drawers suffer wear and damage over the years simply because they are constantly being opened and closed. Loose joints are easily repaired by taking the drawer apart, cleaning out the old adhesive and regluing the bits and pieces. As when repairing any other type of furniture, it is better to leave sound joints alone and to tackle only the weak ones. Most drawer fronts are held to the sides with dovetail joints, which can be hard to separate. If necessary, tap the sides

away with a wooden mallet.

In old drawers, the bottom is generally made of thin boards glued together edge to edge. Sometimes these boards split, either because they cannot take a load or because they have shrunk. Replacing drawer bottoms is not always easy, because they are usually set into grooves in the sides. In other words, you will have to dismantle the drawer in order to fit a new bottom.

Drawer stops are often dislodged by the

drawer being dragged over them. This is inevitable if the drawer runners have slipped or have become distorted. If you detect that a drawer is snagging on its stops, repair the damage as soon as possible. If the drawer is allowed to slide across the stops, its bottom may get broken and this will be difficult to put right.

Drawer knobs are sometimes easily pulled off. Whatever you do, do not resort to wrapping scrolls of newspaper around

REPAIRING A BROKEN DRAWER

1 If the side of a drawer has been damaged, you will have to fit a replacement. First, dismantle the drawer and clean up the joints.

2 Saw a new piece of timber to the correct width and mark the positions of the joints by holding it against the drawer front.

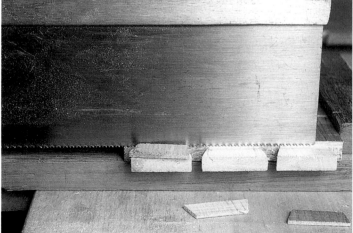

5 You may have to narrow the depth of the joints. Do this using a tenon saw with the workpiece gripped in a vice.

6 Cut out the waste wood, again using a tenon saw. Be careful not to overdo the sawing.

the shaft of the knob. This will most likely enlarge the hole and in the long run make the problem worse. A better solution is to refix the shaft in place with a gap-filling adhesive. If the hole is still too big, try adding a little sawdust to the adhesive and use it like a filler. If you lose a knob, you will be very lucky to find a matching replacement. One way round this problem is to fit a handle so that the backplate covers the hole. If you decide on this method, fill the hole with standard doweling before you fix the handle in place.

3 Mark the dovetail shapes onto the new side panel and start cutting them out. The best tool to use for this is a coping saw.

4 Shape the joint housings with a sharp chisel. You should be able to do this by hand; i.e., without resorting to a mallet.

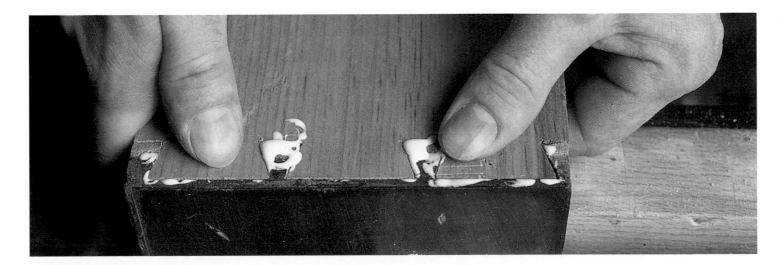

7 When you are satisfied with the shapes of the cut-outs, reassemble the drawer, using PVA adhesive.

Replacing mouldings

Missing mouldings can pose a few problems for the furniture-restorer, as it is not always possible to buy new mouldings to match old profiles. Of course, if you have a multiplane you can make your own mouldings, but this option is not open to all of us. You can get mouldings made from either softwood or hardwood. The most frequently used hardwood is ramin – a honey-coloured wood that is fairly characterless, but is straight-grained and relatively knot-free.

If you cannot find a perfect match for an existing piece of moulding, you may be able to build up a replica using the standard shapes available.

REMOVING MOULDINGS

It is nearly always better to repair a damaged moulding by cutting out the damaged area and replacing it with a custom-made section – however, this is a skilled cabinetmaker's task. The easiest alternative is to remove the entire length and replace it.

Mouldings are usually glued in place, and they may also be pinned. It is not always easy to spot the pinheads as they are often cleverly concealed. To remove a length of moulding, start by levering up one end with a chisel blade. Rest the chisel on a block of wood so that you do not damage the surface of the furniture. If the moulding is obstinate, try applying a little water to soften the glue. It is quite common for the mitre joints at corners to be pinned together as well as glued, so be prepared for this when you reach a corner.

FITTING A REPLACEMENT MOULDING

Having removed the old moulding, clear up any residues of dust, wax or glue. The best way of doing this is with a sharp chisel, but you must be careful not to damage the wood underneath.

After you have prepared the surface, measure up and cut the moulding to length. In most cases, you will have to cut mitres so that the moulding can go around corners. Cutting accurate mitres is not easy, and you will certainly need a good-quality mitre box and a small tenon saw. When measuring up, be sure to take into account the extra length required for the mitres.

Mouldings are usually glued in place. Use PVA adhesive, but sparingly. Some mouldings are also pinned in place. This is not usually necessary, because the pinning does not contribute to the strength of the join, but it is sometimes useful to pin a moulding while the adhesive dries, especially on an overhang.

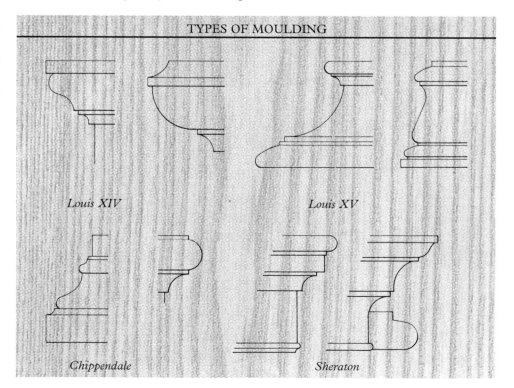

TYPES OF MOULDING

Louis XIV

Louis XV

Chippendale

Sheraton

Left

A 'donkey' is a handy tool if you want to achieve very accurate mitres. The moulding is placed in the slot and the end is finished using a plane.

Above

Planing the edge of a piece of moulding will get rid of the rough, sawn edge. Smooth edges give neater joins.

CUTTING MOULDINGS WITH MITRES

Top left

Clamp the mitre box in a woodworking vice so that it cannot slide about. Make sure of the direction of the mitre, then start cutting.

Top right

Use an off-cut of wood under the moulding so that you can saw right through the moulding without damaging the base of the mitre box.

Replacing skirtings and rails

Skirtings are often missing from chests, and there is seldom any indication of the height or style of the original. Unfortunately there is no way of knowing what the missing part looked like. In such cases, all you can do is try to match the type and colour of the wood and to hazard an educated guess by studying pieces of a similar age and design.

The front corners of skirtings are usually mitred, whereas the back ones tend to be simply butted together. This is because most pieces of furniture which carry skirting are designed to be pushed up against a wall.

Many skirtings are shaped along the bottom. If you want to fit a new, shaped skirting, have a look at a few designs before you start cutting out any wood. To shape the wood, use a jigsaw or a coping saw. Skirting is sometimes nailed or screwed in place, but, thanks to modern adhesives, this is no longer really necessary.

REPLACING MISSING RAILS

A missing or broken rail is not easy to replace, and you need several skills to make an effective repair. The problem is made more difficult if the replacement has to be curved. Some curved parts can be steamed into shape, but this is a highly technical procedure demanding special equipment – steaming and bending wood is usually beyond the scope of the amateur.

Two alternative methods are illustrated here and on pages 76-77. Neither is easy – in both cases a certain amount of experience is required.

HIDING GAPS IN SKIRTING
You may find that when you fit a new skirting in place there are gaps left along the top. One simple and very effective way of overcoming this is to fix lengths of moulding along the top. Stain the moulding to match the colour of the wood before you add varnish or polish.

MAKING A CURVED ARMREST

1 Clamp the piece of wood you want to shape to the sound arm and draw out the profile

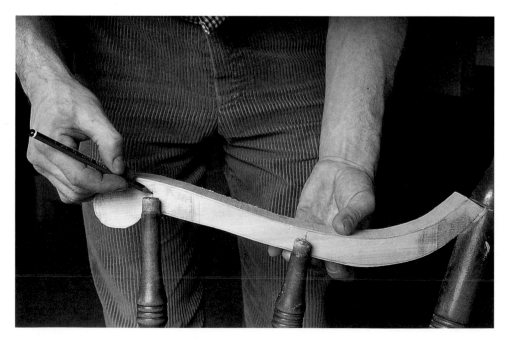

4 Cut the back joint to fit, then pencil in the positions of the other joints.

2 *Use a bow saw to cut out the shape. Always keep to the waste side of the cutting line*

3 *Offer the roughly shaped arm up to the chair and mark off the size and position of the back joint.*

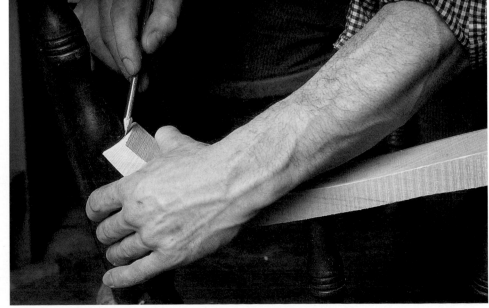

5 *Use an auger bit of the appropriate diameter to drill out the holes.*

6 *Position the arm on the chair once again and scribe out the profile.*

MAKING A CURVED ARMREST (Continued)

7 *Shape the arm using a spokeshave. Make frequent checks to ensure that you are carving the right shape.*

9 *The finished repair. All that has to be done now is to stain and polish the arm.*

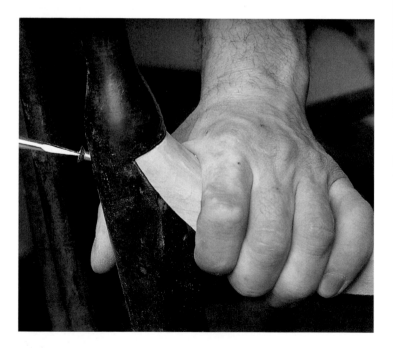

8 *Screw the arm in place from behind. Add glue to the join for extra strength.*

LAMINATING

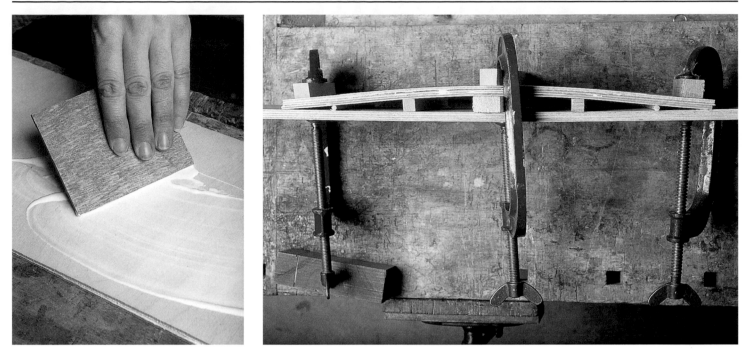

1 Some curved parts can be made by gluing plywood under pressure. Spread PVA adhesive evenly over the sheets that are to be stuck together.

2 Use a collection of clamps to effect the curve. Be aware that the plywood will spring open slightly when it is released.

3 Bend the plywood over small blocks of wood. The size and position of the blocks will determine the radius of the curve.

Restoring a dresser

It may seem surprising, but quite often you come across large pieces of furniture that have pieces missing. In the example illustrated, the top of a dresser was missing. In order to restore the dresser to its original design a new top had to be built. Obviously, a job of this size is no small undertaking, but it is immensely satisfying in the long run.

Before you embark on a large restoration project, it is well worth doing some basic research to determine the shape, design and size of the piece you intend to build. You could visit a library, but a few visits to several furniture shops would be equally rewarding.

Smaller replacement jobs, like making a

new chair seat, can often be done satisfactorily by using bits and pieces taken from old furniture that is beyond redemption. The advantage of doing this is that you can be certain that the wood will be well seasoned. Of course, it may not be easy to match grain, colour and texture perfectly, but this is something that you have to live with.

Building or rebuilding substantial pieces of furniture takes time, and it also often needs extra equipment and space. It is often useful to have a friend to help you work and position pieces accurately.

WHERE TO LOOK FOR OLD FURNITURE

If you are looking for bits and pieces of old furniture that you want to cannibalise, there is little point in spending large sums of money. House-clearance sales often provide cheap furniture. Also consider sale rooms, where many a good deal is to be had. Your local municipal tip is another source of old furniture. Amazingly, unthinking individuals discard perfectly sound pieces of furniture daily.

MAKING A NEW TOP FOR A DRESSER

1 Use new pine or old pine for a job of this kind. Plane down the edges of the side panels first.

2 Check that the edges are square and smooth.

5 When marking up wood, always use a try square to guarantee accuracy.

6 Use a marking gauge to scribe the depths of rebates.

Far left
The base cupboard was
all that was left of the
dresser, but it provided
enough clues for a
designer to draw up
plans for a suitable top
section (left).

3 To save time and to ensure accuracy,
mark the back boards in groups.

4 Having marked the boards, cut them to length
with a sharp panel saw.

7 Saw down to the lines scratched by the
marking gauge.

8 Cut out the waste wood from the rebates
with a sharp chisel.

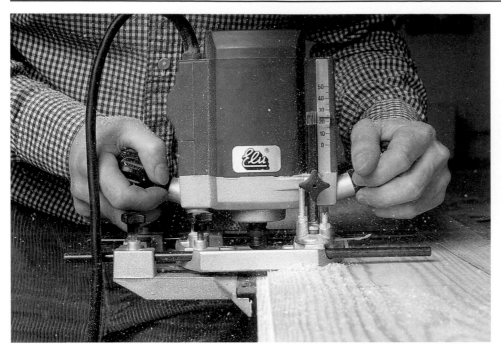

9 *For cutting long rebates, such as those in the side panels, use an electric router.*

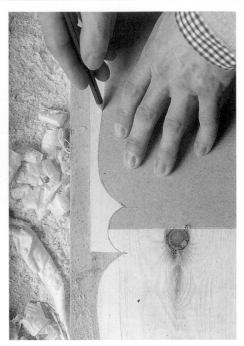

10 *Cut out a card template for fancy designs and use it to mark the panels.*

13 *A chisel is the best tool to use to clean up tight saw cuts.*

14 *Having shaped one side panel, use it as a template for marking the other.*

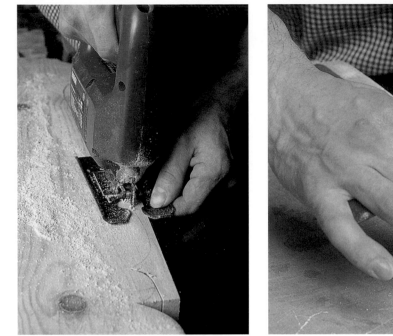

11 *An electric jigsaw makes light work of cutting out shapes.*

12 *Use a spokeshave to tidy up the rough edges left behind by the jigsaw.*

15 *By fitting a different blade in a router you can cut decorative grooves.*

16 *Before assembling the dresser, sand down all the end grains of the boards.*

17 Round off sharp corners on the visible edges of the boards with a plane.

18 Wrap sandpaper around a block before smoothing the boards.

19 Fix the shelf supports with nails and glue. Sink the nailheads below the surface. A filler of coloured wax will help disguise any scars.

20 Before tightening the clamps, check that the frame is square by measuring the diagonals.

21 Use oval nails to consolidate the joints. These nails are less likely to split the wood.

22 Punch the nailheads below the surface of the wood so that they are invisible. A coloured or plain filler or wax stopping will disguise the hole before waxing or polishing.

23 *The finished dresser mounted on top of its cupboard.*

24 *Before varnishing, mix up a stain to match the colour of the cupboard.*

Other materials

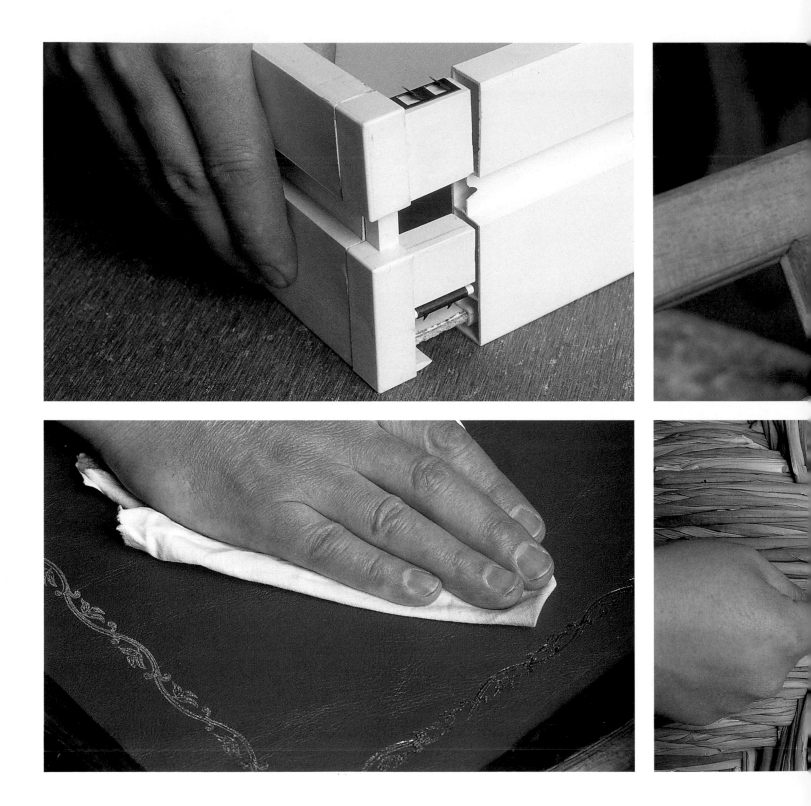

This section is devoted to the restoration of parts of furniture that are not made out of wood – materials from steel and plastic to *papier mâché* and cane are covered. Obviously, different skills and techniques are used on different materials but, by and large, anyone with any aptitude and a modest set of tools can tackle most of the repairs that he or she is likely to encounter.

Only a few of the repair and restoration techniques necessitate special equipment or materials, so provided that you have a reasonable work area you should have no trouble. One thing that is worth bearing in mind, however, is that certain chemicals and paints are potentially lethal if used in confined spaces. For this reason make sure that your workshop has adequate ventilation, especially if you are dealing with plastics. Do not take any risks.

As with any type of restoration work, skill comes with patience and practice, so do not expect a perfect result on your first attempt.

Top left
Repairing a corner on a
plastic drawer.
Bottom left
The finishing touches to the leather
of a relined wine table.
Top right
Replacing a glass panel in a
glazed bookcase.
Bottom right
Renewing a rush seat.

Metals and plastics

Metal hinges, locks and handles are found on all but the oldest and simplest furniture. Tough as most metals are, the passage of time means that wear and damage are inevitable. Directly replacing damaged metal parts would seem to be the easiest way of tackling a problem of this kind, but, in fact, although the commonest patterns of antique hardware are readily available, many of the less usual types of fittings are difficult to find. For this reason some skill at hardware repair is essential for the keen restorer.

Plastics of one sort or another are found in many different types of modern furniture and, because they are easily damaged, it makes sense to know how to repair them.

IDENTIFYING METALS

There are a half-dozen metals commonly found in furniture. Of these, iron and steel are the most used because they are strong and cheap. Steel, although it is often painted over as a protective measure, is silvery-grey in its natural state and may show signs of rust.

Brass is often used in inlays and to make small fittings, like hinges. It is relatively soft and should be handled with care. It is golden-yellow in colour.

Bronze is usually brownish-pink, but it can be treated with chemicals to provide a green or a brown patina. It is a soft metal, and so is used mainly in decorative work.

Copper is a lovely metal; it is rose-pink when clean. Old copper often has a green patina, which can be toned down if necessary. Like bronze, copper is soft and should be treated with respect.

As a rule, aluminium is found only on modern furniture. It seldom corrodes, but it is surprisingly soft, and should be worked on with care.

Silver and gold are rarely found in solid form, but can often be found on antique furniture in the form of plating, to give the impression of greater opulence.

PLASTICS

There are literally hundreds of different plastics and they are not always easy to identify. Bakelite was one of the first plastics to be used in furniture construction; it is sometimes found used for drawer knobs. Unlike modern plastics, it does not burn easily.

Modern plastics – like acrylic sheeting, polystyrene and polypropylene – melt at low temperatures, and this is often the reason why they need repair.

Nearly all plastics can be glued together, but make sure you use the right adhesive.

TOOLS

Metals and plastics can often be tackled with similar tools. For most repair jobs on these materials you should not need a wide range of equipment.

A fine-toothed hacksaw is essential for cutting both materials. A junior hacksaw is probably best for shaping plastics, whereas a large hacksaw is easier to use with metal.

An electric drill and a selection of high-speed (HSS) drill bits are necessary to make holes, and fine files are handy for shaping.

JOINTING METHODS

Both metals and plastics can be moulded and shaped, so jointing is not often required. However, there are many situations where two

or more pieces have to be joined together. There are several ways of doing this.

Sheets or plates of metal are sometimes riveted together. This can be satisfactory, but the rivets themselves can be something of an eyesore. If you want to rivet two pieces together, you will need a special riveting gun to do so.

A neater way of joining pieces of metal together is to use solder. To do this you need a soldering iron, wire solder and flux (flux prevents the solder from oxidising when it is being applied). Soldering does not provide a very strong join, but it can be perfectly adequate for small pieces.

When soldering, you should heat up the metals to be joined; using the tip of the soldering iron, apply the flux and then dab on the solder, which will melt. When the solder hardens, it will consolidate the join. Under no circumstances should you heat the solder directly with the iron – all you will create is a mess.

A third way of joining metals together is to weld them. This requires special tools and equipment and is usually beyond the scope of the amateur restorer.

Plastics are invariably glued together. Some adhesives melt the surfaces of the plastic, which then harden to give a neat and solid join. Most plastic adhesives are inflammable, so take the necessary precautions.

Tools for cutting metals

1 Fine files
2 Electric drill and metal drill bits
3 Electric Jig saw and selection of blades

HANDLING METALS AND PLASTICS

Take care when handling metals and plastics, especially if you are working with sheet materials.

Most metals, especially steel and iron, corrode easily. This can be exacerbated if fingerprints are left on the metal surfaces because fingerprints contain salts that promote rust. So after handling a metal always rub it down with an oily rag.

Plastics are relatively soft and are easily damaged. Acrylic sheeting is sold with a protective layer of paper stuck to it. Keep this paper in place for as long as possible because it prevents the surface from getting scratched.

Metal and plastic fittings

On these pages I have illustrated a few of the huge selection of metal and plastic fittings now available. Many fittings made for modern pieces of furniture are standardised, and you should have little trouble buying them at a DIY store. Old or antique fittings, however, are much more difficult to find. If you want to match such a fitting, the best way is to cannibalise a suitable, cheaply bought piece of second-hand furniture.

METAL FITTINGS

Among the most obvious metal fittings are locks, knobs and hinges, which come in a range of styles and shapes.

Before buying or choosing a fitting, consider what metal you would prefer. Steel is robust, but it is not always very attractive, although you can get black-japanned or polished steels, both of which are easier on the eye. Brass often looks good, but, because it is not very strong, fittings made from it are necessarily simple in design. Needless to say, brass, copper and bronze fittings are more expensive than their steel counterparts.

PLASTIC FITTINGS

Plastic fittings are often specially designed by manufacturers to suit specific products. For example, not all plastic kitchen drawers are the same; if you want a replacement drawer fitting you will almost certainly have to approach the manufacturer.

Plastic fittings, such as knobs and door handles, are often available not only in a variety of shapes and sizes but also in a range of colours. This is one of the great advantages of plastic over metal, especially if you are trying to co-ordinate a colour scheme.

Right
Finding the right fittings for period furniture can be difficult. Sometimes you can adapt fittings bought from your local DIY store, but it is worth making a collection of any old fittings that come your way because they might come in useful in the future.

Far right
Do not be afraid of using plastic fittings. They often offer the best practical solution and nowadays they are both easy to fit and robust.

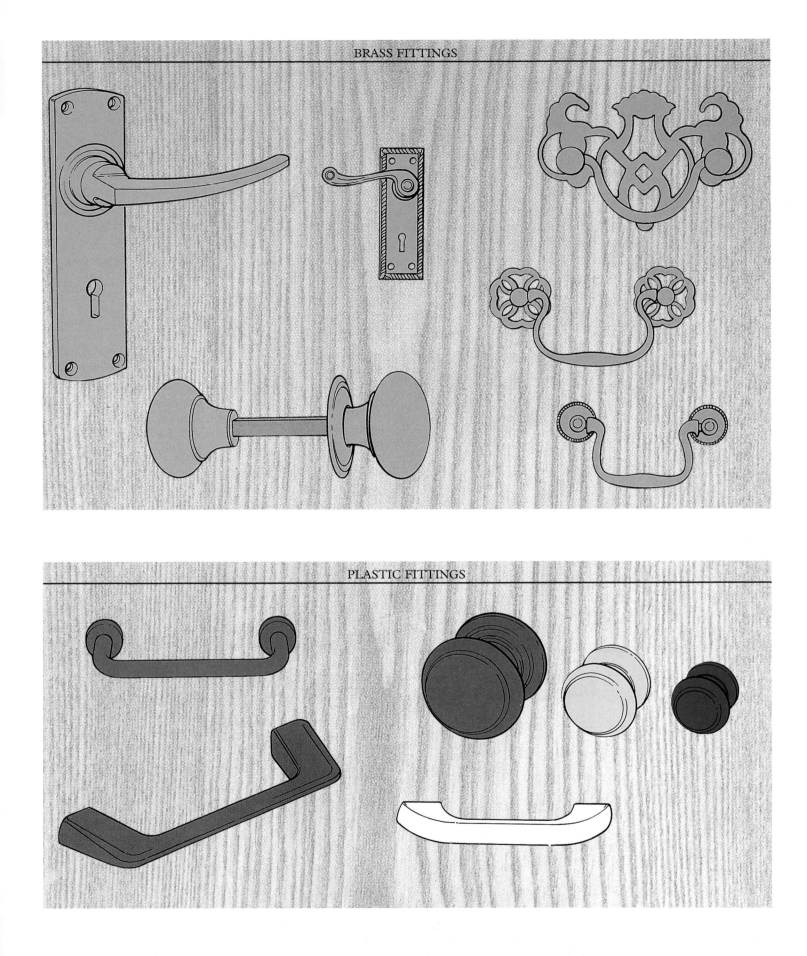

BRASS FITTINGS

PLASTIC FITTINGS

Metal repairs

Although there is an infinite variety of things that can be constructed from metal, the same basic processes are employed in the making of most of them and, if you take your time, you should be able to produce creditable work. One thing that is not so easy to do is to dome or curve metal parts. Quite apart from the fact that you need special tools, considerable skill and practice are required. Always remember when working with metal that any rubbing of metal with metal produces heat, so allow time for the metal to cool before touching.it.

MARKING OUT

If you want to cut out a replacement part, it is best first to make a template which you can use as a guide.

To make a good template, you need a sheet of stiff paper or card. Draw the outline you want on the card and then cut out the shape with a sharp knife or a pair of scissors.

Lay the template on the piece of metal you want to cut and scribe around it, using a hardened-steel point. Press down on the point with sufficient pressure to scratch the surface of the metal.

CUTTING METAL

Before attempting to cut a sheet of metal, make sure that it is securely anchored, as otherwise it will slide around, with the result that you will make a ragged cut. Cut thin sheet metal with a fine-toothed hacksaw, keeping the blade at a low angle so that the teeth do not catch on the edge. If you are tackling a thick sheet of metal, hold the blade at right angles to the workpiece.

FILING AND DRILLING METAL

The file is the metalworking equivalent of the woodworker's plane. It is used to shape metal and to take off unwanted burrs and edges. Files come in many shapes and types, but it is as well to use a good-quality one: cheap ones tend to become blunt very quickly. When using a file, hold both ends firmly and push it across the metal at an angle. Remember that a file cuts as you push it away from you.

There are a few golden rules when drilling metal. The first is to make sure that the piece is anchored, preferably in a special drill clamp. The second is to place an off-cut of wood underneath the metal to protect the worktop and to support the workpiece as you drill through it. The third rule is to mark the hole with a centre punch before you start drilling; if you fail to do this the drill bit may skid, which can damage the workpiece – as well as, of course, being extremely dangerous.

If you are using an electric drill, make sure that the speed is fast. Otherwise the bit may stick, which, again, can be dangerous. Also, ensure that you keep loose clothing and hair out of the way.

If you want to use bevel-headed screws to fix the sheet of metal in place, use a countersink bit to cut away around the hole.

If you are drilling a thick piece of steel, you must keep the bit lubricated or else it will overheat. A mixture of oil and water is the best lubricant, and it should be applied liberally. Thick blocks of metal are best drilled in a drill stand. This practice will guarantee that the hole is straight and is essential if you are using a small bit – without a drill stand, a small bit is quite likely to snap in two.

Sawing metal

Above
Before sawing a thin sheet of metal, anchor it to the workbench with a G-clamp and sandwich it between two off-cuts of wood. When sawing, keep the blade low.

Right
Stout bars of steel are best held firmly in a metalworker's vice. Saw with even strokes and do not apply too much pressure or the blade will stick.

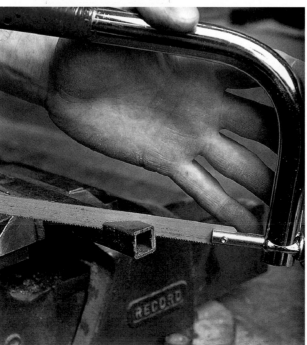

Filling Metal

Top

Clasp the workpiece firmly in a vice, using two off-cuts to provide protection and support. Hold both ends of the file and work it across at an angle.

Above right

Strong pieces of metal do not have to be supported with off-cuts, but they should be clamped in a vice.

Above

Remove burrs and sharp edges with a file. Do this with a minimum amount of pressure or there is a chance that you may scar the workpiece.

Drilling Metal

Right

Before drilling metal, mark the hole with a centre punch – this will prevent the bit from skidding. Also, anchor the workpiece firmly to the workbench.

Far right

When drilling thick bars or sheets of metal, lubricate the drill bit with a mixture of oil and water. This will stop the bit from getting too hot.

Plastic repairs

Plastic furniture is often best repaired using an appropriate adhesive (see pages 93-94), but you may have to cut and shape an insert before you can complete the repair. Most plastics are easy to saw and drill, using a combination of woodwork and metalwork tools. Always remember that plastics are easy to scratch and disfigure, so treat them carefully.

MAKING A TEMPLATE

As with any kind of insert repair, it is as well to make a template before you start cutting and shaping. In many cases, a paper template is more useful than a card one because it can be manipulated around curves if necessary.

After you have shaped your template, transfer the image to the sheet of plastic. If you are dealing with acrylic sheeting, leave the protective covering in place and mark the outline of the template onto it. Leave the protective covering in place for as long as possible.

CUTTING AND DRILLING PLASTICS

Most plastics can be sawn by hand, using a fine-toothed saw. It is not advisable to cut plastic with an electric jigsaw or circular saw because the speed of the blade is such that the frictional heat may melt the plastic, causing the edges to weld back together again even as the cut is being made. If you are cutting acrylic sheeting, lubricate the blade of your hacksaw with soapy water.

If rough edges are left behind after you have cut out the plastic smooth them down with fine wet-and-dry paper.

Plastics are easy to drill using standard high-speed (HSS) bits. Always make sure that the workpiece is secure before you start drilling. If you are using an electric drill, be sure to wear goggles because some plastics are brittle and tiny chips may fly off. For similar reasons, it is a good idea to wear gloves as well.

REPAIRS TO REINFORCED PLASTICS

Some furniture is made from glass-reinforced polyester (GRP) or glass-reinforced epoxy resin. Although these materials are very strong, they are also brittle and occasionally need repairing.

The best way of repairing these plastics is to use the contents of a car-repair kit.

Methods of repair vary, and it is always best to follow the manufacturer's instructions, but with most types layers of fibreglass matting are fixed with an epoxy resin. When using these materials, be sure to protect yourself: they are toxic and give off dangerous fumes. Always wear gloves and, if required, a mask, and work in a well-ventilated room.

If necessary, you can touch up minor dents and superficial damage with an epoxy filler. With these fillers, the two parts are mixed up in the recommended proportions before they are applied to the surface. When the filler has set it can be sanded down flush with the surrounding surface and then painted.

Right
Most plastics can be cut with a fine-toothed saw. Hold the piece steady and saw slowly with firm, even strokes.

Below
Straight edges can be planed down. Hold the workpiece firm in a vice as you work the plane along the edge.

DEALING WITH SCRATCHES
Some plastics are notoriously easy to scratch, and most attempts to restore the surface only make matters worse. Toothpaste, which is a mild abrasive, can be very efficacious in removing scratches from hard plastics.

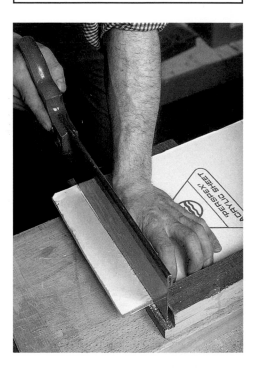

Above

To finish off a straight edge, clamp a sheet of wet-and-dry paper and a square block to the workbench. Run the edge of the plastic over the wet-and-dry paper while holding it tight against the block. Before drilling a piece of plastic, anchor it to the workbench. Drill slowly and wear protective goggles.

REPAIRS TO BROKEN DRAWERS

Drawers made from extruded plastic are found in many kitchens and bedrooms. These drawers are built from hollow, plastic strips, with all the necessary grooves and structural details moulded in place. The strips are joined at the corners by plastic blocks that are usually glued or snapped into place. Damage to such drawers usually arises because they have been overloaded.

Repairs can often be effected by regluing the joints. If you have to reglue all the joints in a drawer, make sure that until the adhesive dries the drawer is held square by means of clamps.

Not all plastic drawers need adhesive for their repair: with some types a replacement piece can simply be snapped into place.

REPAIRING PLASTIC DRAWERS

Below left

Some plastic drawers, or drawers finished with plastic, are jointed at the corners with dowels. If these come loose, replace them and reassemble the drawer using fresh adhesive.

Below right

The corners on some drawers are jointed with sections of extruded plastic. With some types weak joints can be strengthened with adhesive. With others, you will have to get a new section that snaps into place.

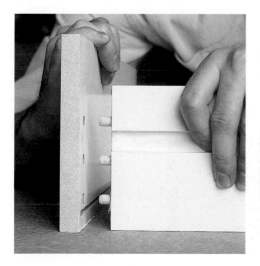

Bending and gluing plastics

In order to make certain repairs to plastic furniture, you have to bend a new insert to fit. Bending rigid plastic is not difficult provided you heat it first and provided you make the curve or angle around a former. Most formers can be improvised from what is to hand - for example, the straight edge of a table or workbench is often perfectly adequate for shaping a right-angled corner.

Thin plastics can sometimes be heated with a hair-dryer until they are sufficiently malleable to be bent. Thicker plastics usually require more specifically applied heat. Assuming you want to bend a sheet of plastic into a right angle, your first task should be to mask off a line about ½in (12mm) wide. The best material to use for masking is cooking foil, as this reflects heat.

Hold the strips of foil in place with masking tape and then play a hair-dryer over the unmasked line. When the plastic starts to become supple, remove the heat and, as quickly as possible, shape the plastic over the former. If the heat from a hair-dryer is not strong enough to affect the plastic, hold the exposed line in front of a radiator. Remember, do not hold the plastic too close to the radiator as many plastics are inflammable.

If you do not want to try your hand at bending plastic, the obvious alternative is to join two pieces together with adhesive. In many respects this is the easier option.

1 Special adhesive is required to join sheets of acrylic together.

GLUING PLASTIC

1 Before gluing one sheet of plastic to another, clean up the edges using a flat sheet of fine wet-and-dry paper.

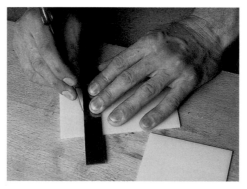

2 Mark a guideline where you want to attach the piece. Use a sharp implement held against a steel straight edge.

4 Position the two pieces together and allow the adhesive to set. Remove excess adhesive with fine wet-and-dry paper.

3 Apply adhesive along the edge to be fixed, making sure that you do not squeeze out too much.

4 Position the piece, and use a square to check that it is at right angles. Hold the piece in place until the adhesive sets.

GLUING ACRYLIC SHEETING

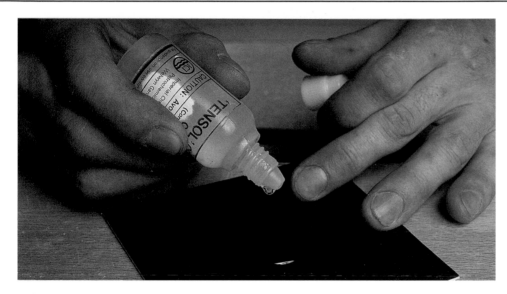

2 *Pour out some of the adhesive onto a mixing board. Card is a good choice, because it will not react with the adhesive.*

3 *Apply the adhesive along one edge, using a pencil or a strip of wood as a tool. Spread the adhesive on sparingly.*

5 *Polish off dirt and dust with a soft, clean cloth. If you want to remove scratches, try using toothpaste as an abrasive.*

6 *If you want to reinforce the joint, drill a series of tiny holes through the repair.*

7 *Cut thin steel pins into short lengths and dip them into the adhesive. Then push the pins into the pre-drilled holes, using pliers.*

Leather and paper linings

Leather covers have been used to protect table- and desktops for centuries. The glazed leather used is impervious to wine stains and ink blots, but it is soft and can quite easily be torn or otherwise damaged. Replacing a damaged leather covering is straightforward – but it is important to use specially prepared leather, which is available in a number of colours. Prepared leather has a uniform thickness and is supple and soft; the upper surface is glazed to add protection.

To replace the leather on a tabletop, you need a steel straight edge and a sharp, handyman's knife. The leather can be stuck in place with a starch-based decorating adhesive.

CLOTH LININGS

The cloth trim found in some drawers and chests serves to protect the contents of the drawer from unplaned wood. Cloth trims are easily torn and they are also susceptible to stains, but luckily it is not difficult to fit replacements. All you have to do is strip away the old cloth and tack or glue new trims in place.

Strip away old cloth by moistening it with warm water – this loosens the adhesive underneath. A flexible stripping knife is a handy tool to have to hand, especially if the fibres of the cloth have started to rot and decay. After stripping off the cloth, sand down the wood underneath until it is flat and even; do not forget the corners, which are where most of the glue will accumulate.

Linen is probably the best cloth to use as a replacement as it is both soft and strong. Cut it into suitably sized strips with a sharp pair of scissors and stick it in place with a diluted PVA adhesive. Turn over the edges of the cloth before you smooth it down with a soft cloth or sponge.

PAPER LININGS

Paper linings were often used instead of cloth. These linings are often very beautiful, but they are fragile and can split and mark easily. Unless the piece is an expensive antique the best course of action is to replace the paper lining.

Strip off the old lining with a flexible scraper and a little warm water. Do not flood the paper with water as this can lead to swelling, cracks and loose joints.

When the old paper has been stripped off, air the drawer or chest in a dry room for a couple of days or so.

Paper for relining work can often be found in interior-design stores. Lining paper traditionally used to be marbled, which is something you can do yourself (see below).

Laying in the new paper is simple enough. Use good scissors to trim each piece to size. Try to have as few joints as possible and attempt to match the pattern. Try the strips for size and, when you are satisfied, paste the inside of the box with lightweight wallpaper paste. Smooth down the paper with a clean, damp cloth or sponge.

1 Peel off the old lining in strips; it should come away easily. Sand down the surface to get rid of lumps and bumps and blobs of old glue.

5 Using a sharp knife held against a steel rule, cut the leather to fit. Try to avoid having to repeat cutting strokes.

CLEANING LEATHER AND CLOTH

Brittle and stained old leather can be cleaned with saddle soap. This is readily available from hardware and riding stores. Old cloth can be revived using a fabric shampoo. When applying the shampoo, try to keep the cloth as dry as possible; pat rather than rub the surface. Very fragile fabrics can be dry-cleaned, provided you sew them into a muslin bag first to protect them from the dry-cleaning machinery. Some old fabrics are now valuable, so it is always best to take advice before you attempt cleaning.

MARBLING PAPER

You can marble paper using enamel paints thinned to the consistency of milk. Put a few inches of water into a plastic bowl and divide the surface of the water in two with a strip of wood cut to fit. Pour three or more colours onto the water on one side of the stick and mix until the paints entwine. Pass a sheet of paper under the dividing stick from the clean water to the paint-covered side of the bowl. Draw the paper up through the paint, adjusting the speed so that you get the right effect. Hang the paper up to dry.

RELINING A WINE TABLE WITH LEATHER

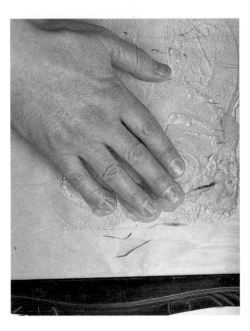

2 Smear a thin layer of wallpaper adhesive over the tabletop. Leave this coat to dry and then apply a second.

3 When the second coat of adhesive becomes thick and tacky, lay on the new piece of leather, firming it into the corners as you work across the table.

4 Use a blunt kitchen knife to crease the leather along the edges of the rebate.

6 If you want to lay a gold pattern along the edge of the table, use gold leaf and a special gilding wheel (see pages 98-99).

7 Finally, clean up any excess adhesive and run over the leather with a clean cloth. To preserve the quality of the leather, treat it with saddle soap from time to time – this will keep it supple and smooth.

Gilding

Gilding is the art of decorating with gold. It is found mainly on fancy mouldings, especially those surrounding elaborate picture and mirror frames. Traditional gilding was laid on gesso, a kind of pigmented plaster. The gesso was built up into shapes and forms and the gold was laid on top. Today it is comparatively simple to touch up damaged gilding, thanks to the large number of gold paints and pastes that are usually mixed with an oil – or wax-based binding. You can even get gilding sticks that work rather like a wax crayon. Of course, few of these touch-up materials contain real gold, but if you want to go the whole hog, you can always use gold leaf. Paints and pastes are usually rubbed or brushed on; some types demand that the surface be primed with size before application. Gold leaf is usually sold in sheets only a few microns thick, so it is very delicate and difficult to handle. It is commonly sold with a backing paper which protects it from damage. Although it is thin, gold leaf is far from transparent. In fact, it adds a touch of elegance and finesse which no other material can match. Gold leaf should be pressed or burnished onto a surface that has first been primed with size.

USING GOLD LEAF

1 Gold leaf is ideal for laying down on soft surfaces like leather where no sizing is required. To lay down a decorative edging, tape down a strip of gold leaf. Try to keep it as flat as possible.

2 Run along the gold leaf with a heated gilding roller. Press down firmly and make sure you move the wheel along a straight line. A straight-edge board is useful as a guide.

GILDING WITH A GOLD STICK

Touch up chipped or flaking gilding by rubbing the stick over the damaged area. The surface should be clean, dry and grease-free before you start. Some gilding materials demand that the surface be primed with size first.

3 Gently lift up the strip of leaf. If you have pressed firmly enough the roller will have embossed the leaf into the surface.

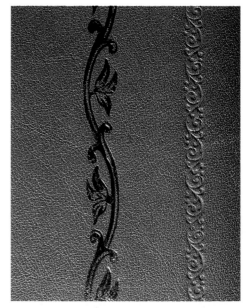

4 The finished effect. A variety of roller patterns are available.

USING TRANSFER LEAF

1 Coat the surface where the repair is to be made with red-oxide primer and sand very smooth. Brush a thin coat of gold size over the primed area and set aside.

2 Transfer leaf is gold leaf on a wax-paper backing. Half an hour after sizing the gilding can be done. Press the leaf gently onto the tacky surface.

3 Use a clean camel-hair brush to pat the gold leaf down against the sticky size. Use fragments of leaf to fill gaps in the coverage.

4 Burnish gently with a pad of cotton wool until the leaf adheres completely. Dip into a little spirit to remove smears.

Glass

Most modern glass is made on a float-glass production line. This gives a product which has little character or texture and which tends to look out of place with antique furniture. For this reason, take great care when handling old glass – buying a suitable replacement piece may prove difficult.

There are several types of glass, so if you plan to replace a broken pane in a bookcase, for example, look around until you find the exact sort you want. Specialist glaziers are more likely to have what you require than a local hardware or DIY store.

TYPES OF GLASS

Different types of glass can vary considerably in quality and strength and so it is worth knowing something about the commonest sorts before you go out and buy.

Sheet glass is quite difficult to buy in small quantities. It is usually thin – ⅛in (3mm) or less – and it is sometimes suitable for use in old furniture. This is because it has ripples and flaws that give it character.

Float glass comes in a range of thicknesses: from a little over ⅛in (4mm) up to 1in (25mm). Glass ⅜in (9mm) thick is commonly found in windows, but glass for tabletops and shelves usually varies in thickness between ⅜in (9mm) and ⅝in (15mm).

Diffuse-reflection glass has microscopic dimples in its surface and these reduce reflections from nearby light sources. This type of glass is often used in picture-framing.

Patterned glass is available in hundreds of different designs and in various thicknesses. However, it is not always easy to find a matching replacement.

Spun glass is difficult to find, but some Arts & Crafts furniture requires the

---

SAFETY
In many countries there are strict laws about the type of glass that can be used for windows, doors and tabletops. It is wise to check before you buy. Your local glazier should be able to advise you on these laws. Never forget that glass can be extremely dangerous and it is always best to play safe, especially if there are children around the house.

---

ornamental centres for decoration. It can be obtained from specialist suppliers.

TOOLS
The most essential tool for glazing is a decent glass-cutter. There are several different types, but a wheel-cutter is as good a choice as any.

To drill glass, you need a special bit with a tungsten tip. These are always used with a lubricant, such as light engineering oil, as they can get very hot in use.

A pair of pliers and a putty knife are necessary if you are replacing a broken pane.

HANDLING GLASS
Always wear gloves when handling sheets of glass. Thin leather ones are ideal – thick ones tend to be clumsy.

When you carry glass, always hold it under one arm; big sheets are best carried by two people – one at each end.

Glass is not easy to cut cleanly, nor is it easy to drill. Life is made much easier if you

can provide a bed for the sheet of glass that you are working on. Thick felt is ideal, but using several layers of newspaper works equally well.

If you want to grind down the edges of a sheet of glass, you would be well advised to have this done professionally. Grinding glass is a skilful business and the cost of having the edges ground for you is well worth it. However, if you just want to round off sharp edges, try running a wet carborundum stone along them.

1 Wheel glass-cutter
2 Tungsten-tipped spearpoint glass drill bit
3 Glazier's putty knife
4 Glazier's plier

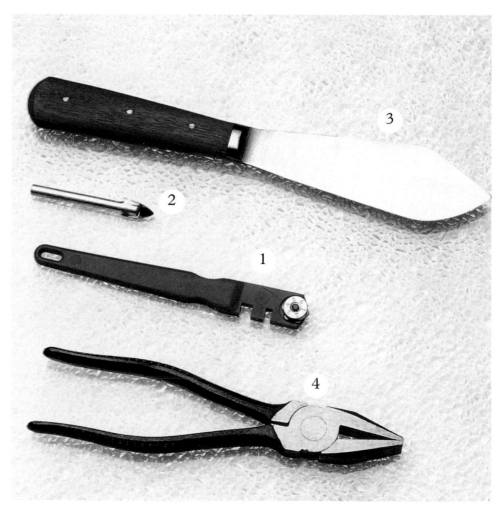

REPAIRING A GLAZED BOOKCASE

1 Remove any fragments of broken glass from the rebate and then make a card template.

2 Lay a sheet of glass on a bed of newspapers and, holding the glass-cutter like a pen against a straight edge, score the glass. Slip the straight edge under the score and press down on the glass to snap it.

3 If you want to cut out a curve you will have to score a line freehand.

4 Mix a compatible stain in with the glazier's putty to match the colour of the wood. The putty must be free of lumps.

5 Line the rebate with putty, rolling it out with your thumb.

6 Push the new pane into the putty and rub off any excess with a finer. On the front of the panel, bevel the putty using a putty knife.

Mirrors and leaded lights

Repairs to damaged mirrors and leaded lights are different from other glass repairs, both because the glass is especially prepared and because it is fixed in a unique way.

MIRRORS

Modern mirrors are generally made from flat glass whose rear has been sprayed with a thin coating of silver. They give a near-perfect reflection, although it is common to find that the reflective coating has been scratched or has started to corrode. Old mirrors, on the other hand, were often coated with a thin deposit of a mercury-tin amalgam. This gives a soft and slightly greenish cast to the reflection.

On the whole, it is best to avoid trying to touch up a damaged reflective surface. For one thing, the chemicals used are often toxic and contain substances like mercury, arsenic and lead. If you want to have a mirror re-silvered, ask your local glazier, who should be able to help or give advice. It should be remembered that very old glass should be re-silvered only after you have taken expert advice, since the repair may reduce the value of the piece to collectors.

LEADED LIGHTS

Leaded lights are made up of regular or fancy-shaped panes of glass held together by strips of lead whose cross-section looks like an 'H'. This was the traditional method of making windows from small, handmade panes of glass. Individual panes can be replaced quite easily, although you may have to improvise a few tools.

1 Although it may appear to be difficult to replace a broken pane in a leaded light, the job is surprisingly easy.

Left
Typical of the colour and condition of old mirrors is this fragment laid on an elaborate, reproduction mirror. Note that the softer colour of old mirrors has been achieved in the reproduction by choosing one of the variety of modern mirror finishes now available. An even more effective result can be obtained by chemically ageing the modern 'silvering' – although this is a specialist job.

5 Add the depth of the rebate to your drawing and then cut out a pane to fit. Use a straight edge as a guide, and press down firmly on the cutter.

REPAIRING LEADED LIGHTS

2 Remove fragments of glass with a pair of pliers. Try not to distort the shape of the lead strips.

3 Using a blunt kitchen knife, lever up the borders of the lead. At junctions, you may have to resort to using a soldering iron to break the lead free. Use the soldering iron very gingerly.

4 Using the lead framework as a template, mark out the shape of the new pane on a sheet of card.

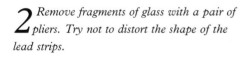

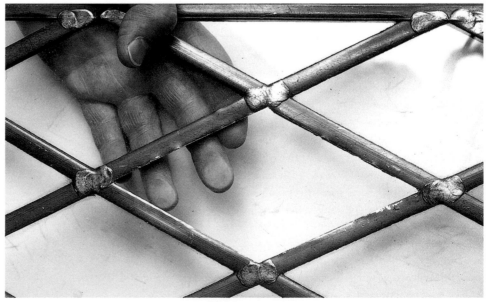

6 Try the new pane for size, making sure that it will fit into the rebate.

7 With the new pane in place, stroke the lead flaps back down again, using a piece of softwood. Press the lead right onto the face of the glass so that the pane cannot rattle around.

Cane furniture

Cane furniture is light, elegant and surprisingly durable. Most of the cane used for making furniture comes from rattan palms, found in South-east Asia and South America. The rattans yield many different kinds of cane, of widths varying from 3in (75mm) down to ⅛in (3mm); the smaller sizes are used to wrap and strengthen joints, whereas the larger ones are used for construction.

Since cane furniture is so diverse, it is impossible to describe all the types and all the various ailments from which they suffer. However, for most people, a cane repair means weaving a new seat or backing for a chair.

PREPARING CANE

Cane should be dampened before it is used. This makes it supple, pliable and easy to work; if you use it dry, it is likely to snap. If you are repairing something like a chair seat, prepare several lengths of cane at the same time. Do this by standing them in a bowl of water for a few minutes and then wrapping them up in a plastic bag or a damp cloth. As you carry on working with the first batch, set about preparing the second, and so on.

As you work a length of cane you may find that it dries out and becomes brittle. If this happens, run a moist cloth along the strand.

TOOLS

Few specialist tools are needed for caning, and most can be improvised from the average toolkit. Some of the tools you may require are mentioned below.

A commander can be made from an old pick handle. It is not an essential tool, but it is useful for straightening cane. Secateurs are handy for cutting pieces of cane to length. For thick sections, use a small hacksaw. A cane knife is used to split and notch thick cane. A square awl is useful for boring small pilot holes for pins because it is unlikely to split the wood. Pliers are essential for pulling cane through holes, and golf tees make excellent pegs for holding cane in holes temporarily.

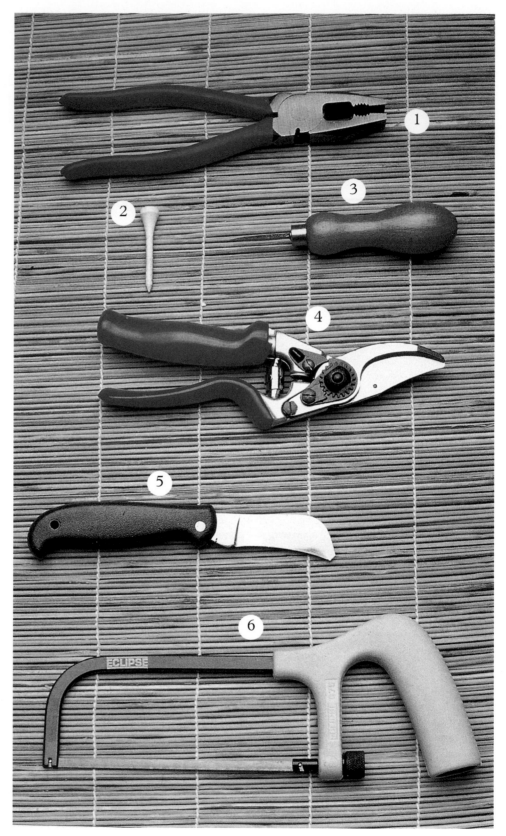

Tools for caning

1 Pliers
2 Golf tees
3 Square awl
4 Secateurs
5 Cane knife
6 Small hacksaw

BENDING THICK CANE

Some pieces of furniture are made out of thick pieces of cane, which require special treatment before they can be bent.

Soak the cane in water for 24 hours before you attempt to bend it. After soaking a length, mark on it where you want the bend to be, then pass the marked section over a blow-lamp flame. As you move the cane over the flame, rotate it so that it does not get scorched. Flex the cane from time to time to test it for softening.

When the cane is sufficiently supple, bend it to shape. You may be able to bend thinner sections by hand, but in the majority of cases you will need some kind of former.

When the curve in the cane is satisfactory, rub a damp cloth over it to cool it down; if the curve needs to be modified, reheat it and try again.

FINISHING CANE

New cane – especially large pieces – can be darkened to match old work by charring it with a blowtorch or by passing it over the flame of a smoky candle. Rub the sooty deposits into the cane with a cloth. Obviously this treatment has to be done carefully or else the cane may catch fire.

If you want to paint cane, wipe it down with turpentine first; if you do not do this the paint will in time flake off. The easiest way to paint cane – especially if you are painting woven work – is using an enamel aerosol. Before using an aerosol paint, make sure there is adequate ventilation and stand the workpiece on layers of newspaper.

USING PRE-WOVEN CANE

In some types of furniture, cane is used as decoration. For example, some tables have panels of cane which are supported on sheets of plywood. The simplest way of repairing this type of canework is to buy a mat of pre-woven cane. These mats are readily available in a number of sizes and designs from specialist suppliers.

Before laying down a mat of cane, soak it first in warm water and then cut it – oversize – to the approximate shape you want, using sharp scissors or secateurs.

Prepare the surface of the panel by stripping off any old cane and any residues of adhesive. If necessary, colour the backing board with wood stain.

The simplest way of fixing a mat of cane is with a staple gun or with small tacks, but this may look very unattractive and the mat may work loose in time. A better way is to brush a diluted solution of PVA adhesive over the backing board and lay the damp mat of cane on top. Smooth the cane with a clean cloth, but try not to disturb the weave.

Before trimming the mat to size, allow it to dry out thoroughly, because it will shrink slightly as it dries. Trim the surplus with a sharp knife and cover the edges with lengths of binding cane or with beading; these can be glued or stapled.

Left
Cane seats and backs on old chairs are almost always stretched and sagging. The only way to restore a chair is to replace the canework. Shown here is an example of a newly caned chair.

Caning chairs

REPAIRING A CANE CHAIR

1 Cane seats and backs on old chairs are almost always stretched and sagging. The only satisfactory way to repair them is to replace the canework.

2 Using a sturdy craft knife, cut away the old cane, following the inside line of the frame. Take care not to damage the wood.

3 A fringe of old cane will be left around the edge. Pull out the strands using pliers and clean up the frame with a damp cloth.

7 When the first layer is complete, the end of each length of cane should be anchored with a golf tee.

8 The second layer is laid on top of the first; there is no need to start weaving at this stage.

4 Drill out the peg holes around the seat. Make sure the drill bit you use is the same size as the old holes. You can use an electric drill for this, but it is easy to damage the wood.

5 After removing all the scraps of cane and the old pegs, check the frame of the chair for loose joints and any signs of woodworm. If necessary, tackle these problems now – later will be too late.

6 Thread the prepared cane, glossy side up, down one hole, across the underside of the frame and up through the next hole. Anchor the cane in each hole with a golf tee before stretching it across to the opposing hole. Build up the first lattice in this way.

9 Working from one corner, weave in the third layer. Each diagonal strand should go over the first pair of canes and under the next. Try to keep the tension even.

10 After the second diagonal layer, the weaving is complete. To anchor the canes, tap prepared pegs into each hole. Sink the pegs below the surface of the wood.

Rush seating

In many rural parts of the world, natural materials have been used to upholster chairs. Of these materials, rushes have proved to be the most satisfactory, although woven-grass seats are also popular.

Today, rushes are harvested in, and shipped from, eastern Europe. Changes in farming practices in the West have wiped out most of the wetlands that provided rushes for thatching and chair-making.

Rush-seated chairs are still manufactured to traditional designs in Poland and Germany, and are gaining in popularity. However, the material is not intrinsically strong and consequently repairs to rush seating are comparatively commonplace.

Seagrass is another natural material. It looks like rush and is sold already spun into a continuous cord, which makes it easier to handle.

New rushes
A wet hessian bag helps to keep rushes in good shape for use. Remember not to store the damp rushes for too long, or they will develop black, mildewed patches.

BUYING AND PREPARING RUSHES

Freshly dried rushes are pale green in colour and gradually change to a pale brown over the years. Dried rushes are packed into bundles; the stems are around 6ft (1.8m) long. If you buy a bundle of rushes, check that they have not been unduly crushed and keep an eye out for signs of mildew.

Before being used, rushes should be soaked in cold water for about five to ten minutes and then left to stand wrapped up in damp towelling for a further four hours. Each stem should be wiped clean and all excess water should be squeezed out.

TOOLS

A rush needle is the only specialist tool required for rushwork. You will also need a sharp knife to cut the rushes and a wooden mallet to beat them down as they are woven.

REPAIRING RUSHWORK

Before you cut away any old rushwork from a chair seat, study the method of weaving; traditions vary from country to country and from area to area. Make a note of the method and attempt to reproduce it as you carry out your repair.

Cut away all traces of old rushwork with

a sharp knife. After this, carry out any necessary repair work to the frame. Finally, bind in the new rushes, following your notes.

REPAIRING GRASSWORK
Repairing a seagrass seat is much like repairing a rush seat. If possible, copy the original weaving pattern. Seagrass is usually wound onto a shuttle, which makes the material easier to manipulate as you pass it through the chair frame.

The old rushes will need cutting away and then the whole frame is repaired, cleaned and repolished before reseating.

RENEWING A RUSH SEAT

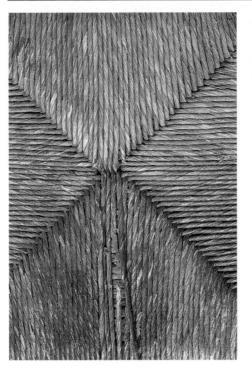

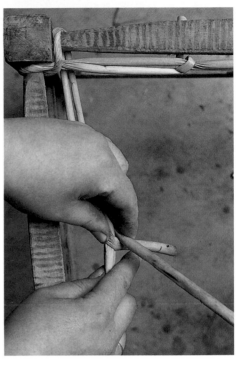

1 Once the rushes become brittle and start to break up there is little that can be done to preserve them. The replacement of the whole seat is necessary.

2 Rushes are used in pairs. Start by tying one end of a pair to the inside edge of a seat and then, twisting them together, wind them round the seat in the pattern shown.

3 Rushes are half-hitch-knotted to the end of each pair as the work proceeds. Keep twisting them as you work, ensuring that the twist is even on the visible parts. Where a pair *of rushes is too thin to give an even appearance to the growing seat, a third rush can be simply twisted into the cord to increase its bulk.*

RENEWING A RUSH SEAT (Continued)

4 As the work proceeds, the short ends of the rushes begin to stick out all round the seat. These can be tucked inside or clipped off.

5 Make sure that the rush forms a regular pattern on the surface layer. Irregular seats will need extra turns of rushes at the wider parts.

8 As the 'hole' in the centre of the rushing gets smaller, pushing the packing in is more difficult. Keep pushing in smaller clippings.

9 The final turns are put in using a special rush needle. If the end of the weave is away from the centre of the seat, reverse the twist of the rush.

6 *Push packing cut from dry rush into the spaces between the top and bottom layers as the seat grows. Never use damp rush for packing.*

7 *When the rushes dry and shrink – after 24 hours – a packing stick is used to push the padding home and to press the turns closely together.*

10 *The last rush is pushed in with the rush needle and tied onto the end of the nearest strand opposite. Clip stray rushes from top and bottom.*

Papier mâché and plasterwork

Papier mâché – a mixture of shredded paper and glue or varnish – seems an unlikely choice of material to be used in furniture-making, but in fact it is surprisingly strong and has survived the test of time. Chairs, tables and smaller items, like trays and snuff boxes, have all been successfully made out of *papier mâché*.

CARING FOR *PAPIER MÂCHÉ*

Papier mâché is a very tough material; most problems arising with it are to do with the surface decoration rather than with the material itself. Decorations were traditionally painted on in oils or inlaid with mother-of-pearl and then varnished. Over the years the varnish tends to darken and it may even flake and splinter.

To clean up a piece of furniture made from *papier mâché*, first wipe over it with a cloth moistened with a little soapy water. Then remove all traces of soap with a clean rag. The next thing to do is to work over the surface with a wad of cotton-wool lightly dipped in ethyl or methyl alcohol. A final clean with a cloth dipped in turpentine should complete the job.

When cleaning a valued piece of *papier-mâché* furniture it is as well to play safe from the start by trying out each of the three cleaning solutions on an unobtrusive part. It is quite possible that one or other solution may remove a layer of varnish – which is the last thing you want to do!

REPAIRING SUPERFICIAL DAMAGE TO *PAPIER-MÂCHÉ* FURNITURE

Some types of furniture are constructed from wood and then covered with a layer of *papier mâché*. It is with this type of work that superficial damage is most likely to occur because the shell of *papier mâché* is liable to crack as the wood underneath flexes and moves.

As always, there is little point in repairing the surface until the structural work has been dealt with. If possible, reglue joints to stabilise the structure.

Thick layers of *papier mâché* are best repaired using a two-part polyester filler; thinner layers can be built up using scraps of newspaper that have been soaked in a hard-setting wood glue. Whichever method you use, sand the repair down once it has hardened and then touch it up to match the surrounding finish with an enamel or cellulose paint.

REPAIRING DAMAGE TO PLASTERWORK

Decorative plasterwork is often found on picture frames. Plaster is a fragile material and is vulnerable to knocks and scratches. If you want to repair a damaged piece of plaster, you can try modelling a new piece to fit, but this is usually more trouble than it is worth. A more satisfactory method of effecting a good repair is to make a mould of an undamaged part of the frame and then to cast a new section of plaster. This is easily done using an alginate-mould solution – you should be able to get this from a recognised art supplier. Obviously, this method is limited to symmetrically patterned frames.

Left
An example of a papier-mâché *chair*

RESTORING A PLASTER FRAME

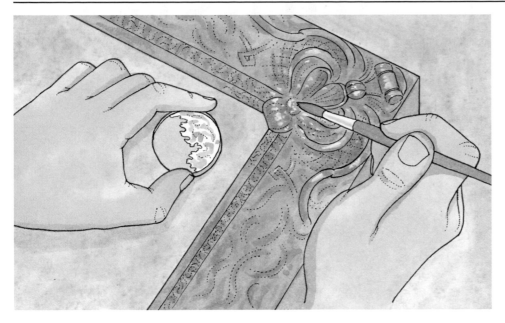

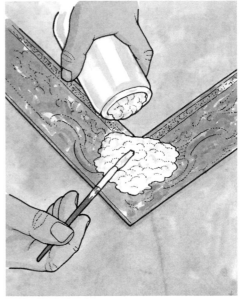

1 Brush petroleum jelly over the area from which you want to take the mould.

2 Mix up the alginate solution, following the manufacturer's instructions.

3 While the mould is still in a semi-liquid state, apply it to the required spot. Press it into crevices and corners, working quickly.

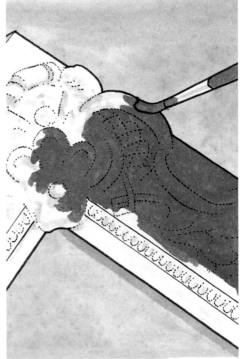

4 When the solution has hardened, lift off the mould and brush it with cooking oil; this will prevent the plaster from sticking to it. Mix up some dental plaster and pour it into the mould. Leave the plaster to set, then remove it from the mould and position it on the frame. Use an old chisel or file to shape the base of the plastercast so that it fits snugly on the frame.

5 Stick the plastercast to the frame with PVA adhesive, and when it has set firm brush on two or three coats of gesso to form a base for the gold-leaf finish.

Upholstery

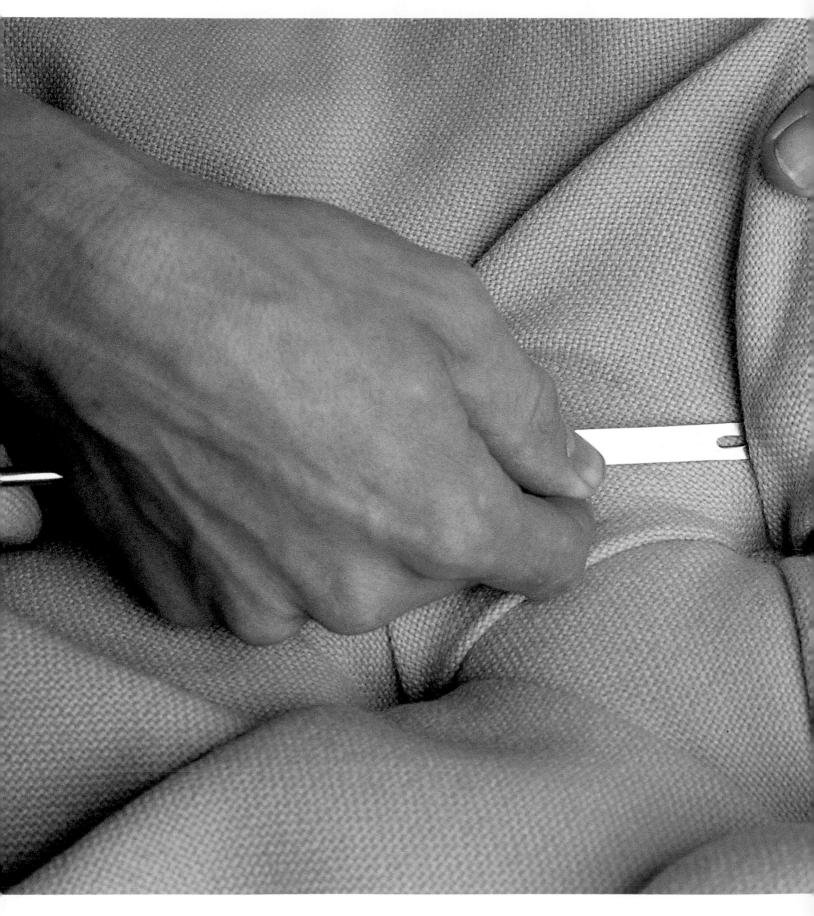

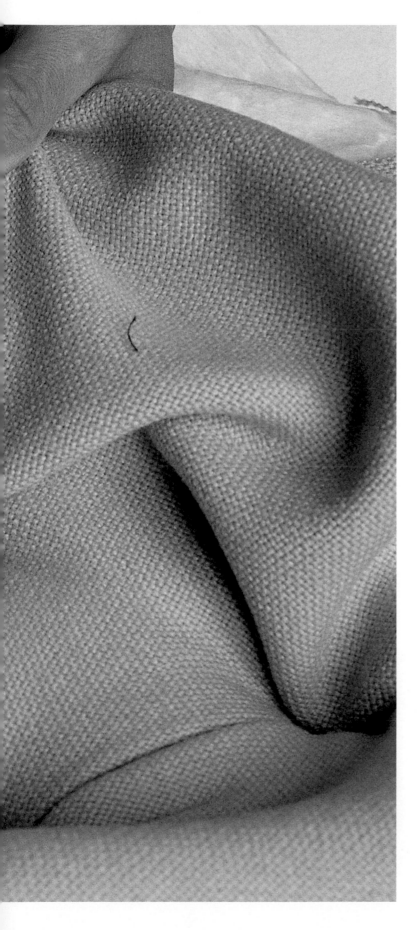

Upholstery can be as simple or as complicated as you like. The term covers everything from a single thickness of fabric on a drop-in dining-chair seat to the advanced techniques needed to deal with a fully sprung, padded and buttoned armchair or sofa.

Upholstery as we know it today began when the coil spring was invented in 1828. Before this, seating was simply padded with horse-hair or fibre and could be rather uncomfortable. Most of the techniques of upholstery were developed during the Victorian era, when large, overstuffed, deeply sprung and buttoned chairs and sofas were popular.

The secret of successful upholstery is to start with small, simple items so that you can learn basic techniques, such as webbing, tacking and padding, and work your way up.

Upholstery demands patience – there are no short cuts to a good finish. Be prepared for the fact that re-upholstering a large piece of furniture, such as a sprung armchair, can take several months rather than a few weeks. Always work slowly and carefully, making sure that each stage is perfect before you begin the next. You will also need a fair amount of physical strength to deal with the larger pieces. All this effort is, however, worthwhile, as even the most unpromising chair or sofa can be transformed by new springs and padding and an attractive cover.

Left
Deep-buttoning a piano stool

Upholstery materials

The materials needed for upholstery (hessian, springs, webbing etc.) are best bought as needed. It is expensive and unnecessary to keep a large stock of anything but tacks (these are always needed). Work out the materials you require before you begin work on the piece of furniture; then you will not have to stop halfway through for extra supplies.

Upholstery materials are graded by quality. Buy the best materials you can afford – poor-quality materials will wear quickly. It is sometimes possible to re-use springs, but only if they are in good condition and not bent or twisted out of shape. Never use old twine or laid cord – it may be rotten in parts and will give way when put under any sort of tension. Good quality is particularly important when choosing fabric for the top covers, as this bears the brunt of the wear and tear.

ESSENTIAL MATERIALS

English 2in (50mm) webbing is suitable for most upholstery jobs. Pirelli webbing can be used to take the place of tension springs.

Hessian comes in many different weights: tarpaulin hessian is used as a spring cover, scrim hessian for first covering and 10oz (280g) hessian for arms and backs.

You will need a selection of twines, cords and threads, including laid cord and numbers 1, 2 and 3 twine.

A selection of ⅔in (16mm) improved and fine tacks, ½in (13mm) improved and fine tacks and ⅖in (10mm) fine tacks will suit most jobs. Impact adhesive is used for foam and braids.

Springs come in various gauges. There are traditional coil springs, tension springs and spring units. Fillings vary from coarse fibre used for the first stuffing to soft Courtelle used as the last.

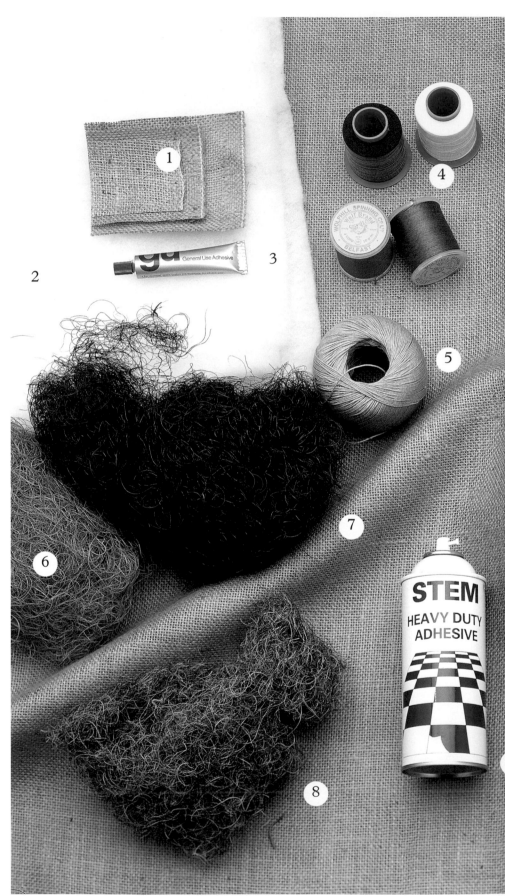

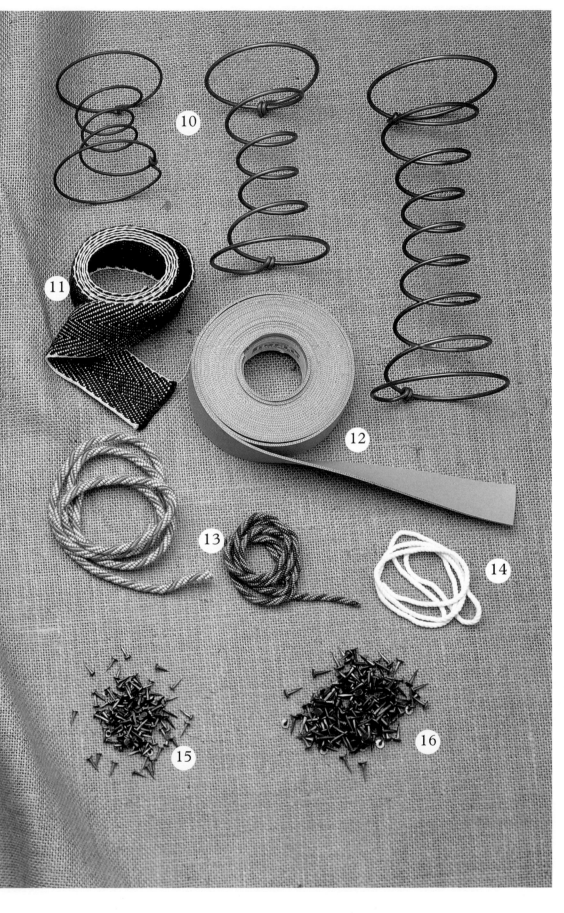

1 *Hessian*
2 *Polywadding*
3 *Clear adhesive for attaching braid*
4 *Threads*
5 *Twine*
6 *Ginger-fibre filling*
7 *Black-fibre filling*
8 *Hair filling*
9 *Impact adhesive*
10 *Traditional coil springs*
11 *English webbing*
12 *Pirelli webbing*
13 *Decorative cords*
14 *Piping cord*
15 *Fine tacks*
16 *Improved tacks*

Upholstery tools

The toolkit needed to begin upholstery is small and reasonably inexpensive. Begin with an upholsterer's hammer with a face about ³⁄₅in (15mm) across and a two-pronged claw. Magnetic hammer heads, which will hold a tack against the face, are also available. As you become more proficient, you will need a cabriole hammer for hammering in tacks close to rebated, polished or carved edges.

Most seating has webbing, so you will need a webbing-stretcher. The bar type is best. A ripping chisel, with either a straight or a shaped blade, and a mallet are both used when stripping furniture. Sharp, good-quality scissors, of either 8in (20cm) or 10in (25cm) size, are another essential.

You will require a number of different sizes of needles. A good selection is: a spring needle (curved for inserting bridle ties and sewing in springs), large and small circular needles, a couple of bayonet needles and a buttoning needle. Skewers (pins 3-4in – 7.5-10cm long – not to be confused with kitchen skewers) help to hold the work in place.

ESSENTIAL TOOLS

A ripping chisel, tack-lifter and sharp knife are all used in removing old upholstery. Cutting-out shears and small, pointed scissors are both needed.

You will need an upholsterer's hammer, a magnetic hammer (this holds a tack onto its face and is handy for awkward corners), a cabriole or two-headed hammet and a heavy hammer. A webbing-stretcher and a batten-and-peg-stretcher are essential. The best type is the hinged-bar type shown here.

You will need long, medium and short mattress needles, a spring needle, semi-circular needles pointed at each end, a bayonet-point needle, a round-point needle, a circular bayonet needle and a cording needle. Other items shown here are a stuffing-regulator, upholsterer's pins and skewers, a steel tape, and a fabric tape measure. Your sewing machine is most probably equipped with piping and zipper foots and will be able to overlock edges.

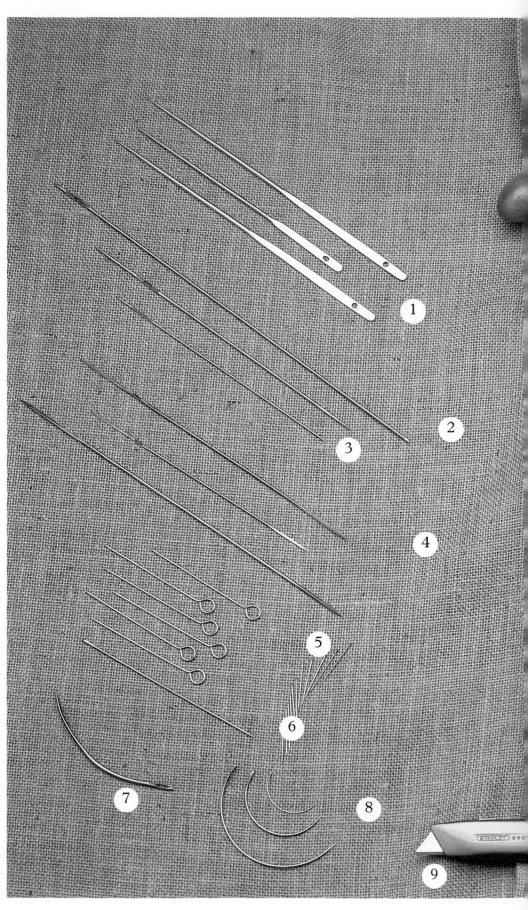

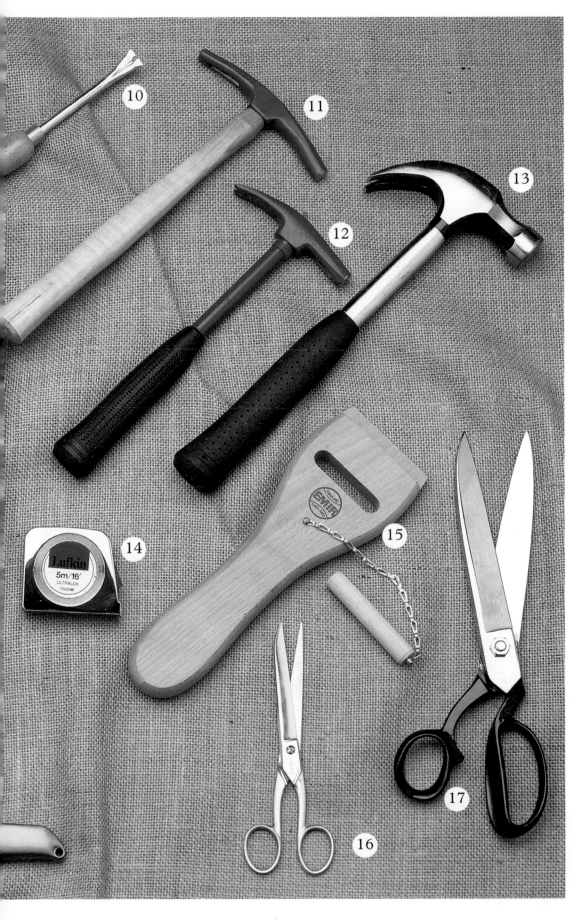

1 Stuffing-regulators
2 Mattress needles
3 Buttoning needle
4 Bayonet-point needles
5 Skewers
6 Round-point needle
7 Spring needle
8 Semi-circular needles
9 Sharp knife
10 Tack-lifter
11 Magnetic upholstery hammer
12 Upholstery hammer
13 Hammer
14 Steel tape measure
15 Webbing-stretcher
16 Small, pointed scissors
17 Cutting-out shears

Stripping old work

Before work can begin on renewing uphol-stery, the old cover and sometimes the stuffing and webbing must be removed. If the stuffing and webbing are in good condition, leave them in place – there is no need to do unnecessary work. All that you would need to do in such a case would be to spread a thin layer of new stuffing over the top of the old material. Have a large plastic bag ready to take the waste material – fibre stuffing will spread itself every-where if it is left lying around. You will need a ripping chisel and a hammer to do the work.

STRIP SAFELY

- When stripping, wear goggles to protect your eyes from flying tacks and wood splinters.
- Always wear stout gloves to protect your hands from sharp edges and old tacks.
- Remove tacks with the grain of the wood. This will help to avoid wood splinters.
- Always work away from you when using the ripping chisel. If the chisel slips it can cause a nasty cut.

STRIPPING

1 Begin by running a sharp knife along the edge of the seat and removing the outer cover.

4 Cut through the ties to free the stuffing. Remove and discard it.

2 Remove the first layer of wadding from the top of the seat.

3 Cut away the calico beneath to reveal the stuffing.

5 Lift the tacks holding the hessian using a ripping chisel and a wooden mallet, as shown here. Pull the hessian away to reveal the webbing beneath. If the webbing is in good condition, leave it.

6 If the webbing is in poor condition, use a ripping chisel to remove the tacks holding it in place.

Fabrics

Tapestry, which is hard-wearing, is usually used on traditional designs. It can be woven in two layers (called quilted tapestry) to give an embossed look. Brocatelle and damask are likewise used for traditional furniture, particularly chaise-longues and couches.

Dralon velvet is suitable for both traditional and modern furniture. It buttons well, comes in many different colours, patterns and textures and is easy to clean.

Tweeds are made from pure wool or synthetic fibres.

The term `furnishing fabric' covers chintzes, plain or patterned heavy-duty fabrics and various manmade fabrics. Furnishing fabrics are used for both modern and traditional upholstery.

Braids are used for trimming edges.

FABRIC-BUYING TIPS
Bear your lifestyle in mind when choosing fabrics. If, for instance, you have small children or pets, fabrics such as delicate damask and brocade are not a good buy! Use fabrics like hard-wearing tweeds, Dralon and chintz instead. Whatever the type of fabric you opt for, take samples of it home and compare them with your existing furnishings before you buy.

1 Patterned heavy-
duty fabric
2 Vinyl (manmade)
3 Modern brocatelle
4 Damask
5 Plain heavy-duty fabric
6 Manmade-fibre fabric
7 Patterned heavy-
duty fabric
8 Dralon
9 Chintz
10 Dralon
11 Tapestry
12 Tweed
13 Decorative braids

Conservation and cleaning

If you look after upholstery it will give you many years of good service. Vacuum upholstery regularly to protect fibres from grit and deal with spills as soon as they occur. It is worth paying for steam-cleaning once a year.

All fabrics are affected by sunlight, so try to keep furniture out of direct sun. This is especially important if you have several matching pieces, because the furniture exposed to most light will fade faster than the others.

Try to prevent children from climbing on furniture. Bouncing shortens the life of springs and shoe buckles can catch and tear cloth. If you have small children it may be worth investing in loose covers – or at least in arm caps – to minimise wear. Sitting on arms or or the backs of chairs or sofas should be discouraged – it eventually distorts the frame.

1 A large hole can be repaired with a patch. Cut away the damaged fabric and cut a patch slightly larger than the hole.

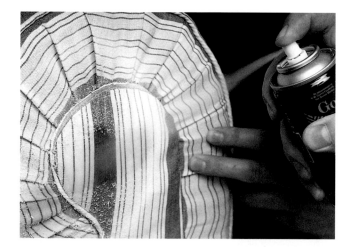

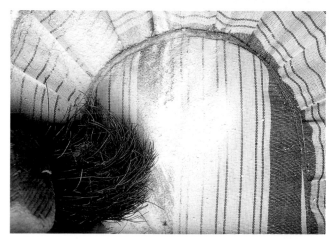

Above
Vacuum upholstery regularly, using the upholstery attachment on your vacuum cleaner. This will prevent dirt from becoming embedded and damaging fibres.

Left
Deal with spills quickly. Mop up the excess liquid with a sponge. Allow the fabric to dry, then tackle the stain with a specialist, dry, upholstery cleaner. If the stain remains, call in a professional cleaner.

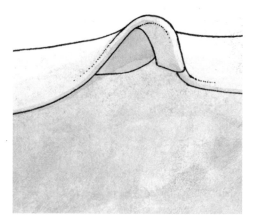

1 Tears that occur close to piping or seams will spread and fray at the edges unless they are dealt with quickly.

REPAIRING A HOLE

2 Turn the raw edges of the patch under by about ¹⁄₁₀in (2.5mm). Press down. Pin the patch in place.

3 Use small, neat stitches in matching thread to attach the patch. Alternatively, use an impact adhesive that is recommended for fabric.

4 When the patch is complete it will be neat and unobtrusive. Whenever you upholster, save some spare fabric in case you later need to patch any holes.

TEARS CLOSE TO PIPING

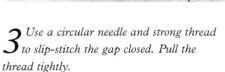

2 Trim any badly frayed edges from around the tear, but do not cut into the fabric. Insert large darning needles or upholsterer's skewers to hold the edges of the tear together.

3 Use a circular needle and strong thread to slip-stitch the gap closed. Pull the thread tightly.

Upholstery techniques

The basic upholstery techniques require very few specialist tools. You can make do with a small or upholsterer's hammer, a selection of tacks, curved needles of various widths and sizes and a webbing-stretcher will be enough for most jobs. A webbing-stretcher is used to tighten the webbing base of seats, and is the only really necessary tool of a specialist nature. Choosing the fabrics with which to replace soft furnishings is the area which is most problematical. Dark fabrics are the most practical for many situations. Remember, it is not possible to wash a cover once it has been tacked in place. Light fabrics are decorative but discolour very easily.

BLIND-STITCHING

1 Blind-stitching is used around the edges of stuffed furniture. Thread an 8in (20cm) double-pointed needle with twine. Insert the needle close to the frame of the piece of furniture. Push the needle so that it comes out about 4in (10cm) from the top edge of the seat and at an angle. Pull the needle almost out.

2 Push the needle back into the seat so that it comes out at the bottom edge ¾in (2cm) to the left of where you began.

3 Make a slip-knot with the two loose ends and pull tight.

4 Insert the needle 1in (3cm) to the right and repeat. When the needle is halfway out, wind the twine on the left three turns around the needle. Pull the needle out.

5 Pull the needle out to form the stitch.

6 Pull the twine left and right to tighten it.

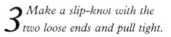

PIPING

1 Fabric for piping is cut on the bias. Strips should be 1½-2in (40-50mm) wide and long enough to go twice around the area that is to be piped.

2 Trim any selvages and join the strips, right sides together, making a ¼in (5mm) seam.

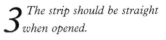

3 The strip should be straight when opened.

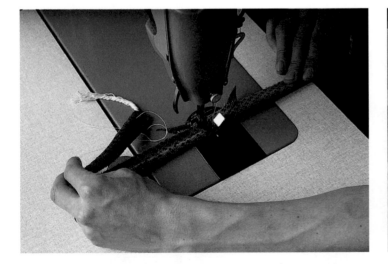

4 Lay piping cord down the centre of the wrong side of the strip, starting about ½in (12mm) from the end. Make a nick in the fabric where the cord begins. Fold the fabric around the cord using a zipper or piping foot and machine along the cord, starting 2in (5cm) from the end.

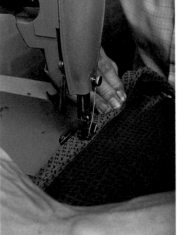

5 To attach the piping, pin it in place with right sides and raw edges together. Machine into place.

6 If done with care, the finished piping should lie along the edge of the seat to give a clean finish.

Loose covers

When re-upholstering an old chair, take the old cover apart carefully and use the pieces to make a template for the new cover.

If you are using a patterned fabric, centre it on the seat and back of the chair. The pattern on the arms should run in line with the inside back. The inside-back pattern should be centred and should match up with the pattern on the seat and front border.

Right

An example of an armchair with completed loose covers.

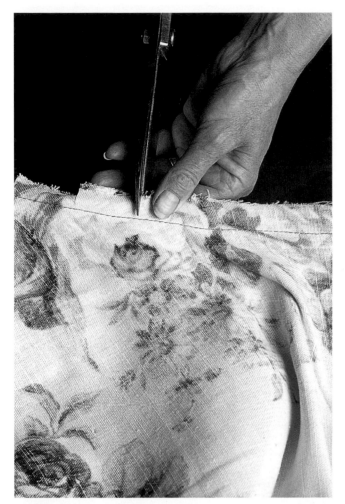

STITCHING LOOSE COVERS

Left
Begin by attaching piping where needed. Pin and tack the pieces of the cover together (wrong sides together). Try the pieces on the furniture before you begin machining.

Below
Snip into curves so that the seams lie flat. Finally, overlock edges with zigzag stitching to prevent fraying.

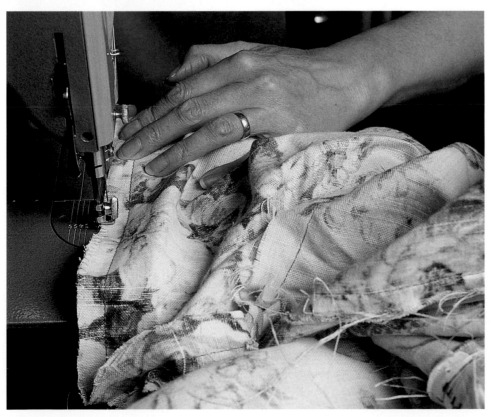

INSERTING A ZIP

1 Turn under a ³⁄₄in (2cm) seam at each side of the zip area. Place the folded edges along the centre of the zip and pin them in place.
2 Using a zipper foot, machine the zip in place. Cut nicks in the edges of the seams so that the zip will lie flat.

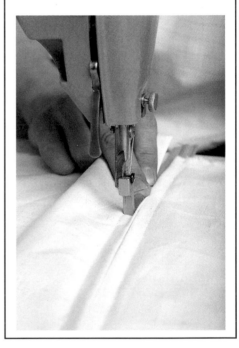

USING VELCRO

1 Velcro is easier to fit to loose covers than a zip, but it does not look as neat in place.
2 Try to fit the Velcro where it will not be seen. The arm parts of a cover can be Velcroed underneath the chair.
3 To attach Velcro, stitch it to the outside of one piece of fabric and the inside of the other so that the two pieces make a join.

A pleated valance

A pleated valance around the base of a chair or sofa is an attractive finishing touch. If you are unsure of your ability to pleat, make a gathered skirt, or one with straight sides and box-pleated corners, as shown below. The frill can be in the same fabric as the rest of the cover (make sure that it matches if you are using a distinctive pattern). Alternatively, it can be in a contrasting or complementary plain fabric. A line of piping in a complementary plain fabric running along the top of the skirt (where it is joined onto the main cover) is a neat, stylish way to finish off.

MAKING A PLEATED VALANCE

1 Measure around the sofa for the length of the valance. Measure the depth to the floor and add 5cm (2in). Double the width around the sofa to allow for pleats. Decide how wide you want the pleats to be and cut a piece of card to this width. Make and pin the first pleat.

4 If wished, pin lining fabric to the back of the valance. This helps it to hang well when attached to the furniture. Use plain white or a colour to complement the main fabric.

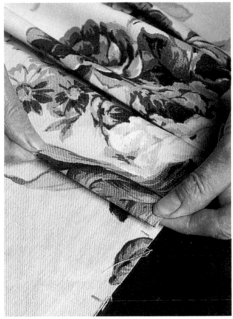

*2 Using the card as a guide, mark the second fold of the pleat.
Pin it in place. Use chinagraph pencil or tailor's chalk to mark
the end of the pleat on the fabric.*

*3 Continue measuring and pleating down
the fabric, tacking or pinning as you go.
At corners, the centrefold of the pleat should
fall on the point of the corner so that the fabric
hangs well.*

5 Machine along the top edge of the fabric.

6 Pipe along the top edge.

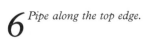

7 *Stitch the valance to the cover.*

Right
An example of a finished pleated valance in patterned fabric.

MAKING A BOX-PLEATED VALANCE

A simpler version of the multi-pleated valance is a valance with pleats at the corners and straight fabric along the sides, front and back. Follow the instructions given here for making this type of valance.

- On a corner of the chair, mark with a pin the point where you want the skirt to start. Measure the distance from the floor. Position pins on the other corners and run a piece of string around between the pins.

- Cut four strips of fabric as wide as the height of the skirt, plus 1in (2.5cm) for turnings. The strips should be as long as each side of the piece of furniture, plus 4in (10cm).

- Cut four pieces of fabric the height of the skirt (plus turnings) and 8in (20cm) long to make the inside of the pleats. Right sides together, sew all pieces along the short ends to make a continuous strip.

- Make a piece of lining in the same way but ½in (12mm) narrower. Sew to the right side of the skirt. Turn to the inside and press well. Pin the skirt to the furniture, lining side out. The centre of each short pleat piece should fall at the corner.

- Pin down each corner so that the skirt fits tightly to the chair. There will be a loop of fabric at each corner. Take the skirt off the furniture and sew each loop down where it was pinned. Press the loop flat and pin it so that there are equal amounts of fabric at each side of the straight, vertical seam to make a pleat.

- Pipe along the top of the skirt. Stitch straight across the pleats at the corners. Pin and slip-stitch the skirt to the cover of the chair.

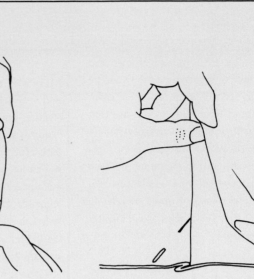

Folding a box pleat

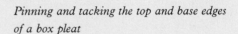

Pinning and tacking the top and base edges of a box pleat

Sofa with box pleat at corners

Inside of box pleat

Box pleat for the corner of a sofa (outside)

Cushions

Cushions can be used to add colour and comfort to a sofa or armchair, or they can be used as basic seating units on their own. Choose the fabric according to the use that the cushion will be put; do not use heavy-duty fabrics. Left-overs from quilts or curtains make wonderfully sturdy cushions; if these remnants are too small for a whole cushion, use them for patchwork or appliqué covers, but make sure that the fabrics are of similar weights and textures.

FILLINGS

Make sure that the filling of your cushion pad is compatible with the outer cover (feather-and-down filling, for example, requires a feather-proof cover) and that the fabric for the pad will not show through.

- Feather-and-down: ideal for loose cushions, scatter cushions and sofa and chair seats.
- Synthetic wadding: lightweight and washable, some of these are allergy-free.
- Kapok: light and inexpensive, it is not absorbent but goes lumpy with use.
- Plastic foam: cheap and useful outdoors.
- Latex and plastic foam: these are made to various shapes, sizes and qualities and are cut to the exact size required.

Lower left
Scatter cushions come in square, round, rectangular and bolster shapes and are used in the backs of chairs and sofas.

Lower right
Box cushions fit comfortably into the chair seat and are usually piped at the top and bottom edges.

Bottom left
Squab cushions are thinner than box cushions and are often buttoned.

Bottom right
Bolsters are used on chaise-longues and Victorian couches.

MAKING A BOX CUSHION

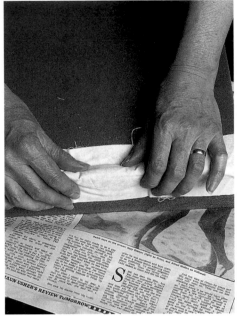

1 Rubber-block foam is best for seat cushions. Cut out the foam so that it fits the seat and mark out a template, allowing ⅖in (10mm) all around for seams.

2 Glue strips of calico to the front edge of the foam. These will be used later to fix the cover to the interior.

3 Lay the template on your material and cut out.

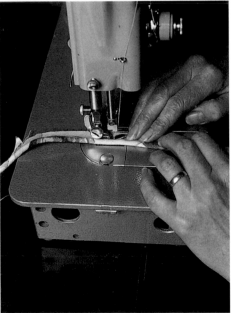

4 Mark and then cut out strips of material for piping and for the sides of the cushion, remembering to leave a seam allowance.

5 Make the piping – see page 127.

MAKING A BOX CUSHION (Continued)

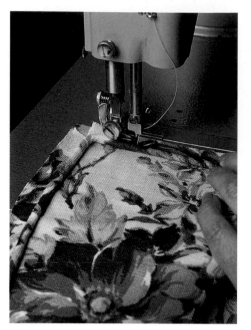

6 Pipe all around the edges of the bottom and top of the cushion. Make sure that the piping does not join along the front edge.

7 When you have piped to within 4in (10cm) of the place where you started, lay the material flat and cut it so that the ends butt. Cut back the piping-cord ends so that they overlap by ¼in (20mm). Stitch the join and then stitch down the piping.

8 Stitch the border to the top panel, using the piping foot and sewing just inside the line of stitches attaching the piping. Continue in this way and stitch on the other panel, leaving the back open so that the foam can be inserted. Check the piped edges on the right side. Overlock the seam edges, using a zigzag foot, so that they will not fray.

9 Turn the cushion cover inside out and place the front border against the front of the cushion. Fix the cover and interior together with skewers. Stitch the calico strip to the front seam of the cover (do not go beyond the piping line). Pull the cover over the foam so that it is right side out. Make sure that all the seams are lying flat. Slip-stitch the back opening.

MAKING A FEATHER-AND-DOWN-FILLED BOX CUSHION

If you are making a feather-and-down-filled box cushion, make a simple box cushion in ticking or other feather-proof fabric. Sew two partitions across the cushion to divide the space into three. Stitch the top panel in place, leaving an opening where each panel falls.

Fill the cushion by hand, pushing handfuls of feathers into the channels. Do not overfill the channels. Machine the seams closed. Use two rows of stitching to make the cushion feather-proof. Make a top cover for the cushion in the same way as the box cover, but push the cushion into the cover rather than gluing it.

MAKING A BOLSTER

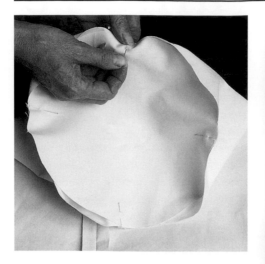

1 To make the inner cover, mark a rectangle on the fabric 1in (2.5cm) longer than the length of the bolster and 1½in (3.75cm) wider than the intended circumference. Machine the long edges, leaving a small gap in the centre so that the stuffing can be inserted. Measure around the end and cut two circles 1in (2.5cm) larger in diameter than this measurement.

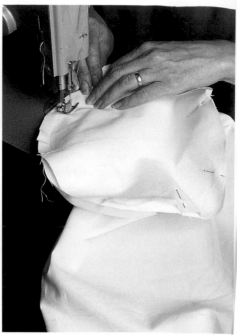

2 Starting at the seam, with right sides together, pin one of the circles to the fabric. Snip into the edges so that they lie flat. Machine the circle to the long piece of fabric. Repeat with the other end. Turn the bolster to the right side.

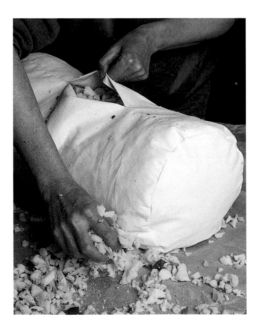

3 Push foam chips into the bolster through the opening in the side seam. The bolster should be firmly stuffed. Slip-stitch the opening closed.

4 Make a top cover, as before. The cover can be piped around the circular edge if you wish.

Frame renovation

If the frame of the piece you are upholstering is in bad condition, it must be dealt with before any other work can be done.

Begin by checking the joints. Chairs undergo many strains and stresses, so there may be some movement. Joints which have started to open should be knocked apart (use a mallet), the old glue removed and damaged dowels replaced and then glued and sash-clamped for 24 hours. There are two types of joints used in upholstery frames. One is the simple dowel joint, with two round pins. The other (usually found on older pieces) is the mortise-and-tenon joint. It is not always possible to take a mortise and-tenon joint apart

to repair it: if you cannot take it apart, reinforce the loose joint and the corner of the frame using steel plates, either flat or right-angled, screwed into place. When using metal plates, ensure that any screws used do not damage existing joints and that the plates are not located in areas that will be required to take tacks during upholstery. For further details of joint repairs, see pages 62-63.

If there are any signs of active woodworm in the frame, it must be dealt with immediately (see pages 28-29).

Reinforcing
A flat, steel, reinforcing plate screwed across the top of a corner will strengthen a loose or damaged joint. Alternatively, a small, wooden, cross member can be fitted, as here, when the angel is not a right angle.

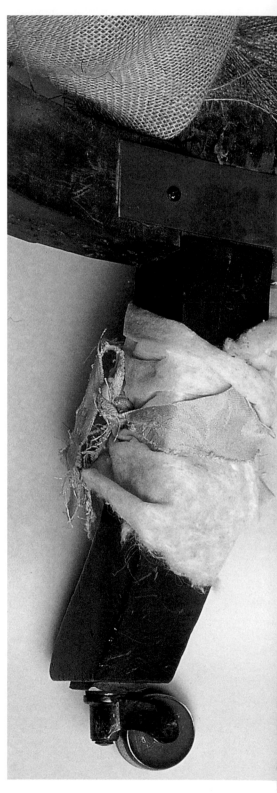

Frame renovation
Almost anything is legitimate for strengthening joints, because brackets become invisible once the chair has been upholstered. This nineteenth-century, round-backed chair needed a metal strip screwed into the frame that would

provide strength to the leg joints and follow the
curve of the frame. Note also that during
frame restoration it is always wise to cover
exposed, polished woodwork to avoid dents
and scratches.

Webbing

Webbing is a lattice of tough, coarse fabric or rubber strips attached to the bottom of a seat or to the back of a chair which acts as a support for the springs and stuffing. When springs are used, they are lashed to the webbing, then the whole is covered with hessian. This assembly is known as a 'spring tarpaulin'.

A webbing-stretcher is an essential tool as it allows you to stretch fabric webbing (known as English webbing) taut and to pull Pirelli (rubber) webbing to the right tension.

It is worth spending time to get the webbing in a piece right. It provides the base of the upholstery, but it will quickly sag and wear if not attached properly.

TRADITIONAL WEBBING

1 Make a 1in (2.5cm) fold at the end of the webbing and place it on the frame, fold uppermost. Fix the webbing in place with four tacks, arranged as shown.

2 Pull the webbing through a webbing-stretcher and pull across to the frame where it will be attached. Fasten with three tacks.

3 Cut the webbing 1in (2.5cm) from the tacks. Fold back and tack in place.

4 The quickest method of webbing an easy chair is to attach three pieces of webbing from back to front, then three more across from side to side on top. Stretch two more pieces from back to front between the first three, then weave two more through from side to side.

USING A WEBBING-STRETCHER

Thread the webbing through the stretcher, as shown below. Pull the webbing through until the stretcher is upright, then, by levering against the chair frame, push the stretcher down until the webbing lies taut. Still holding the stretcher down, tack the webbing to the frame.

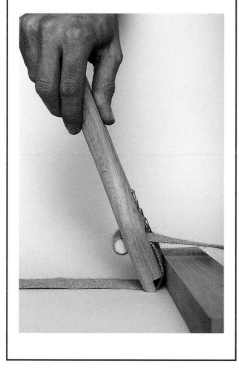

GUNS FOR ATTACHING WEBBING

Experienced upholsterers, or those who intend to do a lot of work, will find a staple or tack gun useful. Both types of guns are available in manual and electric versions. The electrically operated type is the easier to use.

PIRELLI WEBBING

1 Pirelli webbing is usually used as a replacement for damaged tension springs. For seats, use 2in (5cm) webbing; for backs, use 1½in (3.75cm) webbing. The spacing of the webbing should be about 1½in (3.75cm) between each strip.

2 Tack one end of the webbing to the chair frame using four ½in (12mm) fine tacks.

3 Tack the webbing with four tacks and cut off the end of the strip. The tacks must be hammered in so that the heads are flat, as otherwise they may cut the webbing. Tension the first strip of webbing, allowing a 7-10 per cent stretch. Do this using brute force or a webbing-stretcher.

4 Likewise, stretch the other pieces of webbing to the same extent, tack in place and cut off the ends.

Drop-in seats

Most older dining chairs have drop-in seats. The chair has a separate seat, normally a simple wooden frame covered by padding; sometimes seats also have springs supported by webbing. To remove the seat from the chair, undo any small screws or dowels which hold it in place (not all chairs have these – some seats need only a tap to loosen them).

A drop-in seat is a good starting point in learning upholstery, as you will find out for yourself the skills of webbing, simple springing, padding, making stuffing ties, blind-stitching and attaching a top cover.

TRADITIONAL DROP-IN-SEAT

1 Measure the seat with the old covering and upholstery in place. Measure from back to front, as well as from side to side, and allow extra under the seat for turnings.

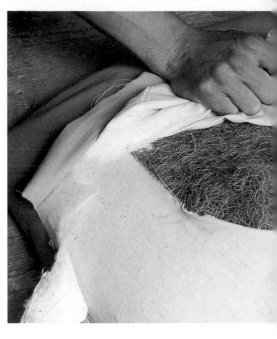

2 Rip off the old cover, check the joints and reweb the seat.

4 Make bridle-stitches across the seat. These will hold the stuffing in place.

5 Make lines of good-quality horsehair stuffing under the bridle-stitches across the seat. Fill between the lines of hair and tease in a further layer of hair to make a domed effect.

3 *Tack tarpaulin hessian over the webbing. Note that an average drop-in seat needs three pieces of webbing from back to front and three from side to side.*

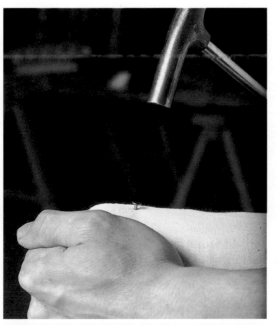

6 *Place the calico over the stuffing. Fold the edges under the seat and temporarily fix in place with a tack at the centre of each side.*

7 *Turn the seat over. Turn the calico to the underside. Temporarily fix beneath with three tacks at the centre of each side and now remove the tacks at the sides.*

TRADITIONAL DROP-IN-SEAT (Continued)

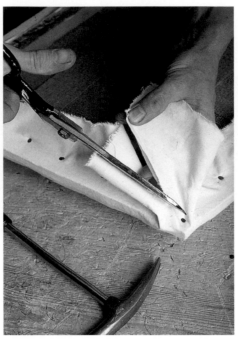

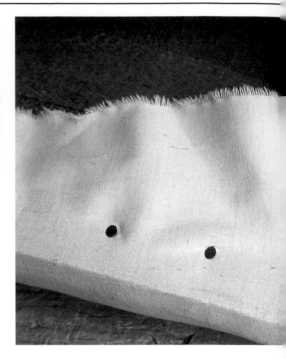

8 Gently pull the calico diagonally at the corners and mitre neatly, tacking in the centre of the mitre. The threads at the centre of the calico should remain straight.

9 Remove the temporary tacks from one side. Stretch the cloth with your right hand and use your left to smooth the stuffing. Smoothing and gently stretching the cloth, tack it in place. Repeat for each side, cutting away spare cloth at the corners.

10 Take care when finishing the mitres so that the corners remain smooth and neat.

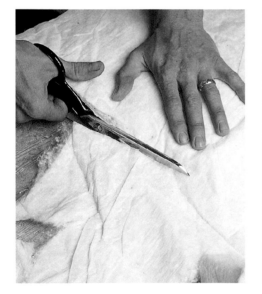

11 Cut a layer of wadding and lay it over the seat of the chair. The wadding should not come over the edges.

12 To attach the top covering, mark the centre of each side of the seat with chalk. Cut a piece of fabric to fit the seat, adding extra for turnings. Find the centre of each side by folding the cloth in half lengthways and then sideways. Mark each centre point with a small nick.

13 Match the nicks to the marked points on the chair. Attach in the same way as the under cover.

MODERN DROP-IN SEATS

Dining chairs made in the 1950s and 1960s often had a plywood base instead of webbing. This was covered with cotton wool, felt or foam. If the plywood is in poor condition, replace it with webbing and make a traditional drop-in seat; if the plywood is in good condition, cut a piece of $^5/_8$in (15mm) thick foam and glue in place. Cover with calico and a top cover.

14 *Complete the underside with a piece of black cloth, turned under and tacked into place.*

Armless sprung chair

These mass-produced modern chairs were made in great numbers in the 1950s and 1960s. Most have a wooden frame with tension springs which stretch from side to side across the back and seat. On some chairs the back cushion is fixed to the chair, on others it is free and rests against the sprung back. Most of these chairs have a loose seat cushion. Provided the frame is in reasonable condition, this type of chair can be given a new lease of life by stripping and restaining the woodwork, renewing the springs and fitting an attractive cover. Working on this simple type of chair will give you an idea of how an easy chair is constructed and will show you the role of the springs before you move on to more complicated, fully sprung chairs with arms (see page 154).

RE-UPHOLSTERING AN ARMLESS SPRUNG CHAIR

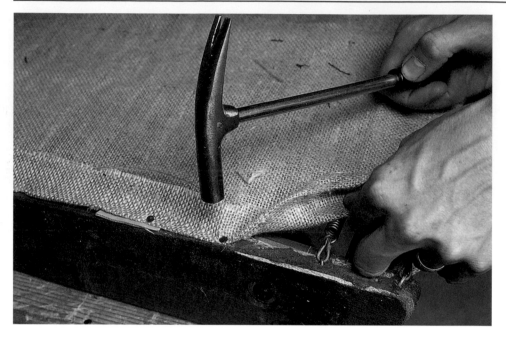

1 Begin by removing the old cushion and covers from the chair. Examine the tension springs. If any are stretched or damaged, replace them with Pirelli webbing (see page 141). Cut out a new cover for the springs and tack in place.

4 To fit the foam, cut strips of calico 2in (5cm) wide; stick half the width of the strip along the two side edges and the bottom face edge of the foam.

2 Remember to include a pleat in the covering material (seen here from the underside) to allow for the stretch of the springs in the seat.

3 Cut a piece of medium-density 1¹/₂in (3.75cm) thick foam the width of the back frame and the same height as the distance from the bottom of the back to the top rail.

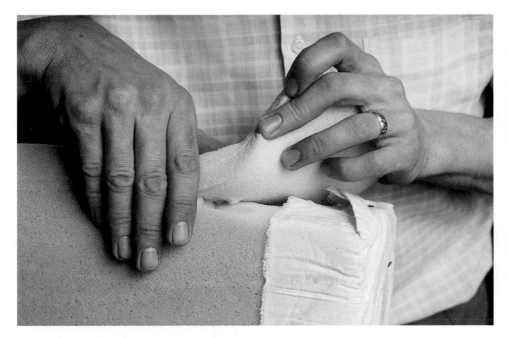

5 When the adhesive is dry, tack or staple the free calico to the frame so that the foam is securely held in place. Then stick ¹/₂in (12mm) foam across the top of the back. The purpose of this foam is to give a soft line to the back so that the hard edge of the frame does not show through the cover.

6 If the chair had a fixed foam seat rather than a cushion, proceed as for the back. Cut the foam, stick calico strips to it and tack into place. The front edge is finished as for the top of the back, to give a smooth and comfortable finish.

RE-UPHOLSTERING AN ARMLESS SPRUNG CHAIR (Continued)

7 *The chair can now be covered. Cut fabric slightly longer and wider than the back or seat of the chair. Cut side and top pieces with the same seam allowance. Wrong sides together, machine the pieces and add piping.*

8 *Pull the machined cover over the back of the chair. Tack the material from behind to the bottom rail of the back, then pull over the rest of the back cover and sew around the edge.*

10 *Stretch the cover over the seat. As you pull the cover into position, make sure that the seam allowances lie flat.*

11 *Once in place, the seat and back covers can be permanently tacked to the frame on the underside of the chair.*

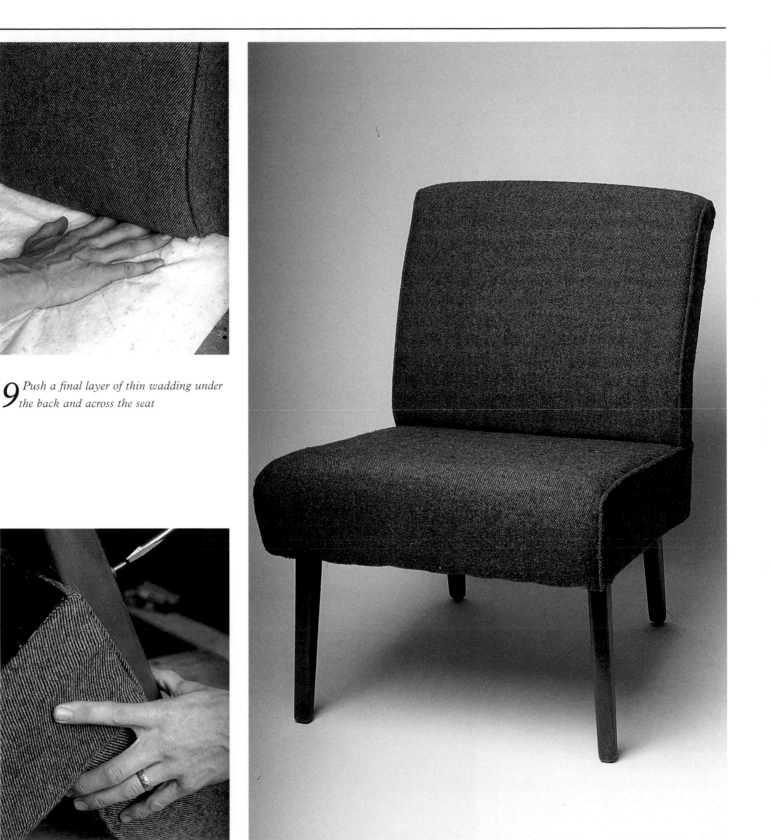

9 *Push a final layer of thin wadding under the back and across the seat*

12 *Finally, cut a piece of black material for the bottom and tack neatly into place. Replace rear legs by screwing through the material into the original holes in the chair frame*

Above
An example of a completely refurbished sprung chair.

Overstuffed seats

Most traditional, good-quality armchairs and some dining chairs have seats constructed by a method called overstuffing. Springs are attached to webbing, covered with fibre, held down by a coarse covering (a tarpaulin) and then another layer of stuffing is added before the final hessian covering.

The processes used in renewing an overstuffed seat are the same as those for upholstering a large easy chair with sprung back and arms (see pages 154-59). Tackling the seat first is a good way to learn before you progress to bigger items. The secret of success is to make the seat stuffing even at the sides and slightly domed in the middle. This may take several attempts, but it is worth persevering. The chair will look lumpy, feel uncomfortable and wear badly if the stuffing is uneven.

When removing the old seat from the chair, make a note of the number and size of the springs and their positions. This will help you to achieve an even, comfortable effect. If the old springs are still in good condition and have plenty of `give', they can be used again. If they are stretched, rusty or broken, buy replacements.

WHAT YOU NEED TO UPHOLSTER AN OVERSTUFFED SEAT

- Webbing: 2in (5cm) is best
- Springs
- Needle
- Laid cord
- Fibre stuffing
- Tarpaulin: 2in (5cm) larger all around than the size of the chair seat
- Tacks
- Scrim: 2in (5cm) bigger all around than the size of the chair seat
- Double-pointed needle
- Strong, medium twine
- Stuffing-regulator
- Thread for blind-stitching
- Hair for top stuffing
- Hessian: 2in (5cm) bigger all around than the chair seat and to fit the gap between the top and lower rails
- Calico: to come over the chair seat and front edge.

UPHOLSTERING AN OVERSTUFFED SEAT

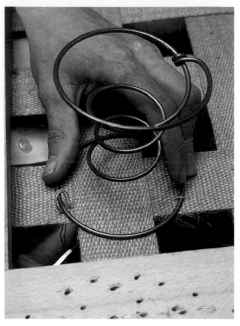

1 Remove the old seat cover, springs and stuffing. Turn the chair upside down and attach new webbing, using tacks (attaching webbing is described on pages 140-41).

2 When the webbing is in place, the springs can be sewn in. Place the springs in position on top of the webbing, centring them where the webbing crosses.

5 Cut a piece of tarpaulin 2in (5cm) larger all around than the area to be covered. Turn the back edge over 1in (2.5cm), raw edge up. Tack all along the back and sides, smoothing out excess fabric. Now stitch the

springs to the tarpaulin. Do this in the same way as stitching springs to webbing (see page 140)

3 To attach the springs, make a slip-knot, then stitch through the webbing, over the spring and back through. Make a single knot, then take the twine to the next piece of webbing and repeat the operation.

4 When all the springs are in place, they can be lashed.

6 Bridle-stitch across the seat in rows. The loops should be loose enough for you to be able to slip a hand under.

LASHING

- Measure from the side edge of the frame, over the top of the springs to the opposite edge. Add half the length and cut to this measurement as many pieces of laid cord as there are rows of springs.
- Put a ⅝in (15mm) tack in the frame where the first row of springs starts. Knot the length of laid cord to the tack, leaving an end which will stretch from the tack to the first spring in the row. Hammer in the tack firmly.
- Hold down the first spring with your left hand so that it is compressed as far as possible. Make the first knot using a hitch on the coil of the spring second from the top. Make the second knot (this time a half-hitch) on the top coil.
- Take the cord to the next spring and knot first on the top coil, using a hitch, then on the second coil nearest the frame with a half-hitch. Continue lashing in this way. Central springs should be tied on both sides of the top coil.
- When you reach the other side, tap a tack in the frame and knot the cord onto it. Tie the loose ends at each side to the top coils of the springs.
- When all the springs are lashed from side to side, lash from front to back, making knots on the top coils. Where cords cross at the centre, twist the free cord around the one already fixed. Springs over 8½in (22cm) deep should be lashed in the middle, as well as the top. Follow the method described for lashing, but tie to the middle coils.

UPHOLSTERING AN OVERSTUFFED SEAT (Continued)

7 *Starting at the back, tuck a handful of fibre stuffing under the loops. Work forwards from side to side. To get an even layer, gently tease the handfuls of stuffing into one another. Use more stuffing in the centre to dome the seat.*

8 *Cut a piece of scrim to cover the seat plus 1¹/₁₀in (2.75cm) all round. Pull it over the stuffing and temporarily tack in place. To hold the stuffing in place, stitch stuffing ties through the seat. Use a double-pointed needle and strong twine. Start 4in (10cm) in from the* sides with a slip-knot and make big stitches across, down and then across again. Press down firmly on the seat. Pull the twine tightly, then tie the loose end around the last stitch. Hammer the tacks home.

11 *Now make the stitched edge, which gives the front of the cushion a neat, firm shape. Start edge-stitching ¹/₂in (1cm) above the blind-stitching. To edge-stitch, insert the needle, push it up through the top of the* chair and push it back in about ³/₄in (2cm) to the left to form a stitch. One or two rows of stitching is usually enough for the average chair.

12 *Bridle-stitch the seat, as described for the first stuffing, and add a second layer of fibre stuffing, as described for the first stuffing.*

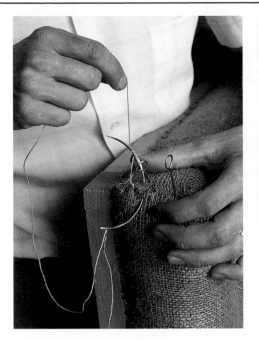

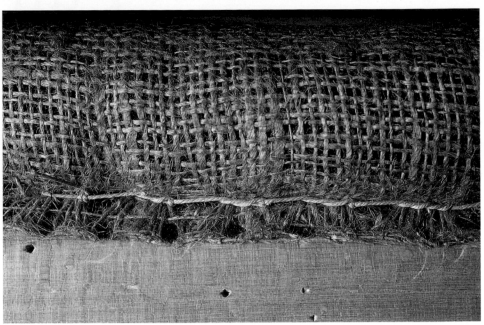

9 *Pull the cover tight at the corners, pin and sew up using a semi-circular needle and twine. Even the stuffing by pushing the point of the regulator in a few inches and moving it back and forth. Repeat across the seat and down to the edges.*

10 *Blind-stitch all around the seat, as described on page 126, and regulate again.*

13 *Cut a piece of calico to cover the seat, pin and then sew in place. The front border can then be bridle-stitched,* *stuffed and covered with calico as before, and the seat recovered with a material of your choice.*

Fully sprung easy chair

THE SPRUNG ARM

A fully sprung easy chair has a sprung seat, with independently sprung front edge, arms and back. This type of chair is one of the most comfortable available – and one of the most difficult to upholster. Do not attempt this sort of chair until you have tried an over-stuffed seat (see pages 146-49).

It is worth buying really good-quality hair and wadding for this sort of chair, as it stops the top cover from wearing too quickly.

Not all of these chairs were stuffed with hair. Some were stuffed with rag flock, wool or alva (a type of seaweed). Many of these fillings are now hard to find, so use hair and wadding instead.

When working on this sort of chair, start with the arms, then do the seat (see pages 156-57), then the back (see pages 158-59). If parts of the chair are in good condition, leave them alone. If, for instance, the seat needs re-upholstering but the back and arms do not, leave them.

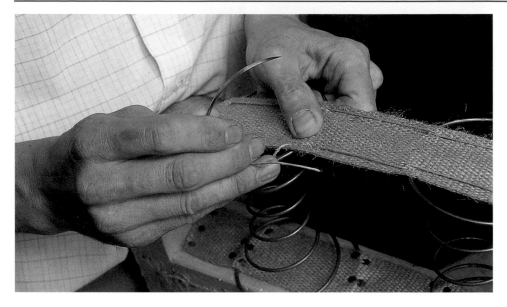

1 Tack two pieces of webbing to the frame. The piece nearest the back should be folded in half and tacked about 2in (5cm) from the frame edge. The other piece should be placed about halfway along the arm, stretching from the top to the bottom rail. Tack a piece of hessian over the inside of the arm frame. The springs used for chair arms are usually 5in (12.7cm), 12-gauge springs lighter than those used for seats. Tack the springs onto the upper part of the frame, then thread a piece of webbing through the lower coils and tack it in place. Stretch a piece of webbing over the top of the coils from front to back and tack at each end of the frame. Sew the top coils to the webbing at four points to prevent too much movement.

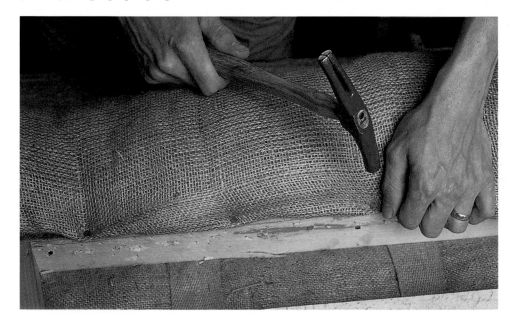

5 Cover the stuffing with scrim tacked temporarily to the arm frame.

2 Lash the springs with three lines of lashing right along the arm. Start with the centre line. Hammer a tack into the inside-back frame upright, knot the twine around it and fasten each spring across the top coil at front and back. Attach two other lines of cord in the same way. The springs should be just above the level of the front of the arm.

3 Cut a piece of hessian 3in (7.5cm) longer than the arm and wide enough to stretch from the bottom rail over the springs and back to the bottom rail on the outside, plus a 2in (5cm) edge. Starting at the inside, tack the hessian along the lower rail, pull it over the springs and then over to the other rail. Tack in place. Stitch the spring webbing to the hessian with rows of blanket-stitch.

4 Sew bridle-stitches across the hessian and start stuffing with fibre.

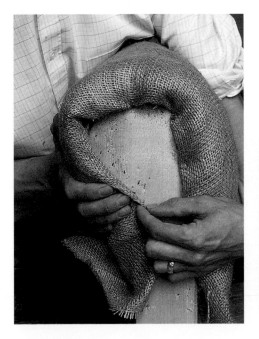

6 Roughly form the shape of the scroll arm and temporarily tack at the front.

7 To hold the stuffing in place, stitch stuffing ties through the arm. Use a double-pointed needle.

THE SPRUNG ARM (Continued)

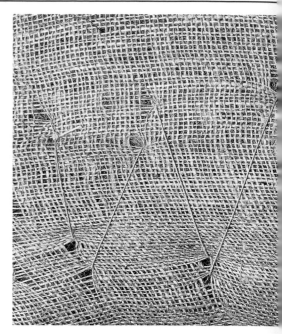

8 Start 2in (5cm) from the front with a slip-knot and move the needle through the arm and back again, forming a zigzag along the length of the side.

9 Pull the twine tight and tie the loose end round the first stitch. Now regulate the stuffing to form the shape of the arm and sides.

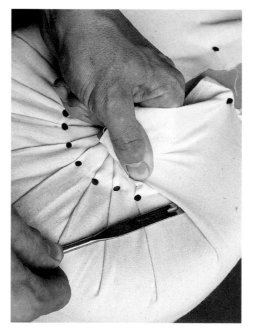

12 Add a second stuffing in the same way, or cut a piece of thick wadding to fit around the arm, as shown here.

13 Next, cover the arm with calico. Tack the calico at the back, on the arm rail and on the side rail. Draw the calico over the front of the arm, pleat and tack in place around the scroll.

14 Now cover the arm with the material of your choice, with piping and pleated front as before. Cut a piece of thin wadding to make a padded covering over the tacks and down the front of the arm. Cover this with your material and pin into place.

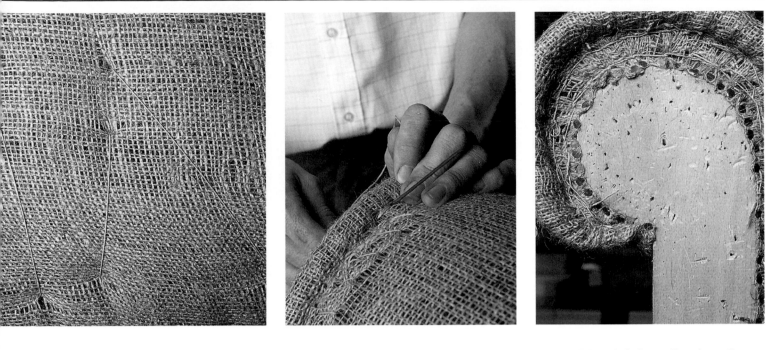

10 Tack the front of the arm permanently and make two rows of blind-stitching to form the scroll.

11 Edge-stitch the scroll to give a firm and neat shape.

15 Finish off by stitching the front together, using a semi-circular needle.

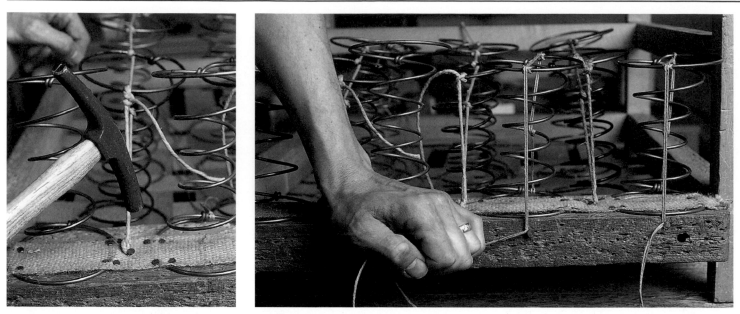

1 *Spring the main part of the seat, as described for the overstuffed chair (see pages 150-53). The spring canvas should be large enough to come right over the front edge and form a 'gutter' between the main part of the seat and the independent sprung edge.*

2 *Place a row of 6in (15cm), 8-gauge springs level with the front edge of the frame. Fix the springs and attach a webbing strip, as described for the sprung arm (see pages 150-53).*

5 *Lash all the springs in this way. Lash a length of cane, which must be pre-bent to shape (you can get this done at an upholstery suppliers), or a piece of heavy-gauge wire to the top coil of each spring, using several turns of twine around each spring.*

6 *Because the front edge is independent from the seat, there must be a gutter between the seat and the front edge. To hold the gutter in place, tack a piece of webbing to one side of where the gutter runs. Pull this webbing taut and tack on the other side.*

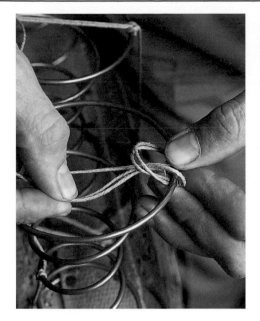

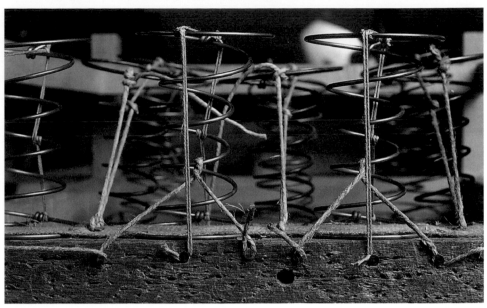

3 Put a ²/₃ in (16mm) imperial tack on the inside of the front rail, directly behind the first spring. Attach a length of laid cord to the tack and hammer it in. Take the cord up through the spring and knot it on the inner side of the middle coil. Take it to the inner side of the top coil and knot again.

4 Bring the cord through the spring, down to the outer side of the middle coil, and knot it. Go down to the bottom coil, knot it, and then up the outer side to the top coil; knot again.

7 Fold the hessian back over the webbing. Make holes through the hessian between each spring. Thread a length of laid cord through the hole and tie it to the horizontal webbing with a slip-knot. Make two such ties between each spring and tack the free ends to the top of the front rail to hold them in place.

8 Pull the hessian over the front springs, fold the raw edge under and tack it to the front rail. Use medium twine to catch the top coil of the springs and the cane or wire to the hessian. Make a stitched edge, as described for the overstuffed seat (see pages 150-53).

THE SPRUNG SEAT (Continued)

9 Bridle-stitch the whole seat and insert fibre stuffing, as described for the overstuffed seat (see pages 150-53) Cut scrim to fit right over the seat from back to front edge, allowing 1in (2.5cm) to tuck under.

10 Fold the scrim under by ½in (1.25cm) and fix it temporarily by tacking along the centre of the top of the back rail. Pull the scrim over the stuffing and tack it to the side rails. The scrim threads must be straight from back to front and side to side.

11 Starting at the centre front, fold this scrim under and tuck it beneath the stuffing on the front edge. Hold in place with skewers.

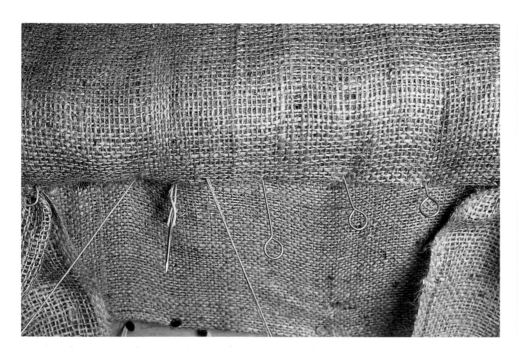

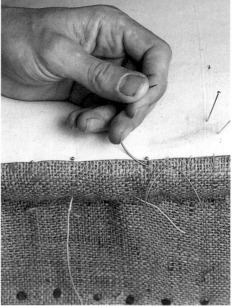

12 Sew stuffing ties through the seat and then blanket-stitch the scrim to the hessian. Continue as for an overstuffed seat (see pages 150-53) until the point where the chair is covered with calico.

13 To cover the independent edge with calico, pull the calico over the edge and, using strong twine and a circular needle, stitch through the calico into the front edge with long running-stitches. Pad the front border section with fibre and secure the cover with stuffing ties, as for the overstuffed seat (see pages 150-53).

THE SPRUNG BACK

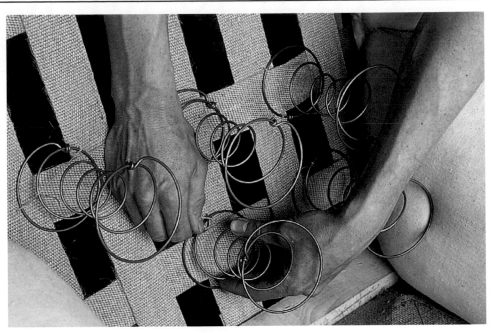

1 Start at the bottom rail and space vertical strips of webbing. Weave in four horizontal strips of webbing, with two close together at the bottom and the other two more widely spaced above the level of the arm.

2 Sew springs in place, as described for the overstuffed seat (see pages 150-53). Use 6in (15cm), 10-gauge springs at the bottom and 7in (17cm), 12-gauge springs above.

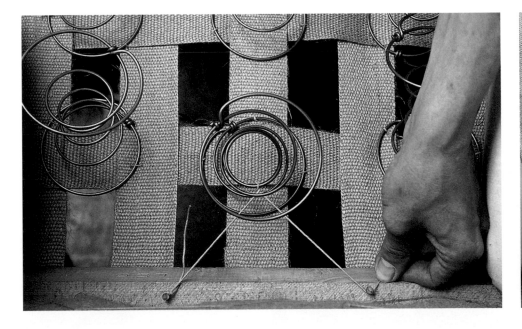

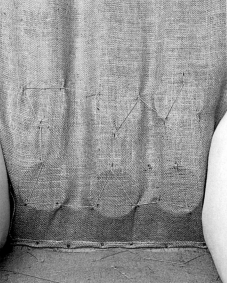

3 Lash the bottom row of springs, as described for an overstuffed seat, pulling the bottom row down towards the seat. Do the same on the next row of springs, but attach the first tack to the side rail rather than the bottom. If you want further rows of springs higher up the back, they should be lashed together and to the top rail.

4 Cover the back with scrim, tack in place and stitch the springs to it, as before. Stuff and stitch the back, as described for the overstuffed seat. When the second stuffing is complete, cover with calico.

Traditional wing chair

Wing chairs have been popular since the reign of Queen Anne. In those days, many great houses were uncomfortably draughty, and the high wings gave the chair's occupant protection against chilly winds.

Traditional wing chairs have a sprung seat, sometimes with an independent sprung edge, and a sprung back. In some, the arms are sprung; in others they are padded. The chair is usually stuffed with fibre and hair. Modern wing chairs usually have tension springs across the back and seat and a foam filling and so are easier to repair than the traditional model.

In most traditional wing chairs, the understuffing on the arms and wings is in good condition and can be left as a base for new top stuffing. Usually, the seat and back must be resprung. If the actual structure of the wings is damaged, it is best to ask an expert furniture-restorer to deal with the chair rather than try to tackle it yourself.

UPHOLSTERER'S TIP

When taking the old fabric and stuffing off a frame, always keep a record of the order in which they were removed. This will prove invaluable when you come to reinstate the new materials; you simply reverse the process!

COVERING MATERIALS

Wing chairs are traditionally covered in velvet, brocade, damask or leather. Multi-patterned, chintz fabrics should not be used, as the shape of the chair makes it difficult to match the design. Unless you are a very experienced upholsterer, steer clear of leather, which is expensive to buy and difficult to work with.

RE-UPHOLSTERING A WING CHAIR

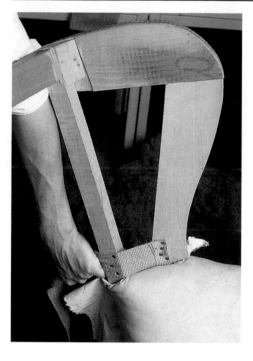

1 To pad the wings, tack webbing across the bottom of the wing and attach a strip vertically to the inside of each wing frame.

2 Cut hessian one-and-a-half times larger than the wing areas and temporarily tack it to the wing, starting along the inside front of the wing rail. Temporarily tack the open, long edge along the inside face of the back rail. At the bottom, pull the hessian to the outside and tack. Bridle-stitch the inside.

6 Continue smoothing and regulating until you have a good, firm shape and tack permanently in place.

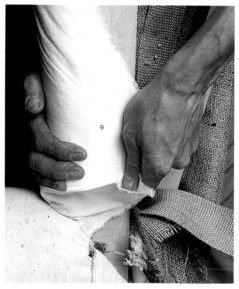

7 Cover the inside of the wing round to the outside of the roll with wadding. Push the wadding through the back rail and cut the wadding so that it fits neatly around the rail. Cover the wing with calico and tack in place.

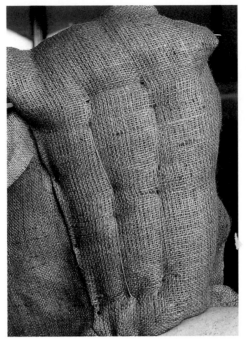

3 Stuff the inside until the surface is smooth and thick.

4 Pull hessian over the stuffing and tack temporarily along the top, front and back of the wing. Insert stuffing ties.

5 Now, using the regulator, tease the stuffing over the top and front rails.

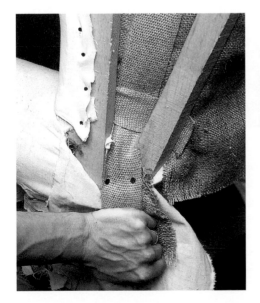

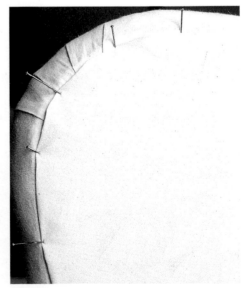

8 Pull the webbing tight and tack it permanently in place on the outside of the arm rail.

9 Pull the hessian through the back and round the side of the wing. Tack in place.

10 Finally, cover the outside with wadding and calico. You can make a clean top edge by tacking a strip of stiff card under the seam.

Deep-buttoning

Buttoning is used largely for decorative reasons these days, but originally it was a shaping device. The diamond effect rapidly became popular as a decoration and was reflected in wall-panelling and fabric design.

There are two types of buttoning: float and deep. Float-buttoning does not give the characteristic, pleated-diamond effect of deep-buttoning and is usually found only in modern and some Victorian upholstery.

Deep-buttoning needs patience and skill. It might be better to attempt a simpler task, such as a headboard or a small, button-backed chair, before attempting a complex task, such as the rebuttoning of a Chesterfield sofa.

Preparation is the secret of successful deep-buttoning. The measurement of the spaces between the buttons, and the marking of where the buttons will fall, must be accurate. It helps to make a detailed sketch of the original work before you start. Measure the position of the original buttons, the spacing between them, the depth to which they were pushed into the filling and the depth of the seat from the front edge to the point where it meets the base of the back. Remove the original covering carefully: doing so will help you to see where the new buttons should fall.

MARKING OUT

Cut a sheet of 3in (7.5cm) foam to the size of the surface to be buttoned. Using a felt-tipped pen, measure across the widest part and mark the middle. Draw a vertical line through this point. Use a compass to mark the centre with a circle. Mark the foam into diamonds. Draw horizontal lines at equal intervals. Mark a point 3in (7.5cm) in from each side of the centre vertical and then mark along the horizontal at 6in (15cm) intervals. Using a straight edge, draw diagonals through the lines from left to right and right to left so that they cross. The points where the lines cross mark where the buttons will fall.

COVERING BUTTONS

There are many different types of upholstery button. The best type to use is the one with a soft pad back, as this allows the button to be pulled deeply into the padding. You can buy a professional buttoning machine (as shown above) to make your own covered buttons at home, but this is not really worthwhile unless you intend to tackle a large quantity of deep-buttoned upholstery very quickly. For a small piece, using less than 20 buttons, it is cheaper to have the buttons covered professionally at an upholsterer's.

VAN DYKING

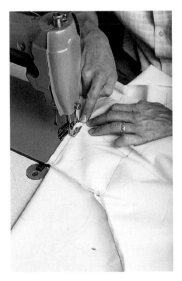

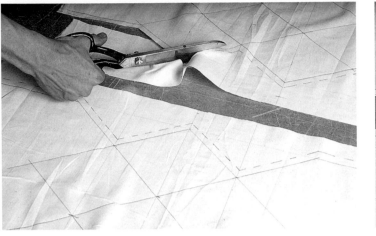

1 To Van Dyke, allow one piece of fabric to overlap the other by over half the width of the planned diamonds and mark out the diamonds on both pieces.

2 Cut out the shape of the diamonds along the edges, about $^1/_2$in (12mm) from the marks to allow for the seams.

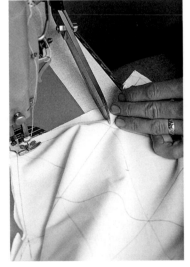

3 Pin the pieces right sides together, along the line of the diamonds, and snip through the seam allowances so that it will lie flat when opened out.

4 Machine together, stitching to the button marks.

5 This simple method of joining will result in an invisible seam when deep buttoned. Here it is viewed from underneath.

DEEP-BUTTONING A PIANO STOOL

Padded and buttoned stools are traditionally covered in velvet. More modern stools are often covered in one of the acrylic velvet fabrics, such as Dralon. In fact, any hard-wearing furnishing fabric can be used. Avoid a densely patterned fabric as this does not work well with buttoning.

1 Cut the base for the seat in ¾in (2cm) thick chipboard. Cut a piece of foam the same size as the chipboard. Mark out the foam and the board into diamonds, as described on page 162.

2 Choose a piece of piping slightly larger in diameter than the buttons that you plan to use. File the edges of the pipe to make a hole-cutting tool.

BUTTONING TIPS
- When working with velvet, or any pile fabric, the pile must run downwards. You will find Dralon easier to work with than 'real' velvet.
- Always do covered buttons at the same time so that they will match.

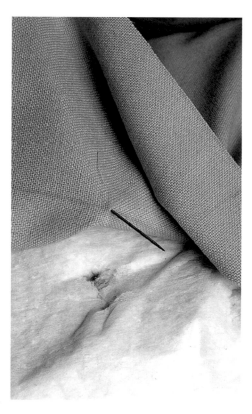

6 Push a mattress needle eye-first through the centre hole on the back of the seat, then through the centre button mark on the fabric. Thread a length of button twine through the needle, thread the button on and then thread the other end of the thread through the eye of the needle. Pull through to the back of the board.

7 Tap in a tack just to one side of the centre hole. Wind one end of the button twine around it, pull the other end of the twine tight and push the button from the right side until the shank touches the board. Wind the end of the twine around the tack and hammer it in.

3 *Punch holes at each button point. Bore holes in the underside of the chipboard to match. Cut the fabric for the cover and mark it into diamonds.*

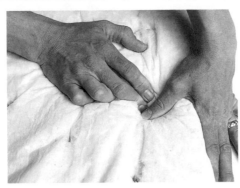

4 *Cover the foam with wadding and tear small holes at each buttoning point. Extend the wadding 2in (5cm) over the edges.*

5 *Cut some 12in (30cm) lengths of button twine and set aside. Have the buttons close to hand.*

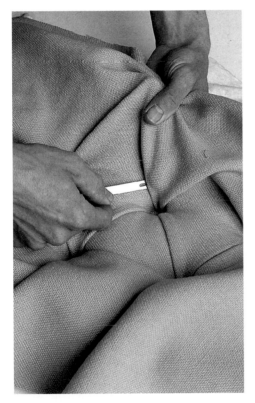

8 *Continue until all the buttons are in place, working away from the centre. Use the flat end of a stuffing-regulator to turn the pleats so that they face downwards. Continue adjusting the pleats with the stuffing-regulator so that they all lie flat. Check carefully before you turn the fabric to the back of the board.*

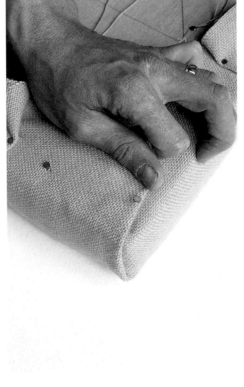

9 *Turn the excess fabric to the back of the board. Mitre the corners and tack the fabric in place.*

10 *Replace the drop-in seat in the stool. Adjust pleats again if necessary.*

GLOSSARY

Aluminium oxide
A long-life grit for abrasive wheels and papers.

Alva
A type of seaweed that was used for stuffing upholstered chairs.

Animal glue
The traditional glue used by cabinetmakers. It comes in toffee-like sheets or in pearls.

Ash
A wood similar to hickory in colour and qualities, which bends well when steamed.

Backflap hinge
Essentially a butt hinge, but with wider leaves so that it can take a greater load. Backflap hinges are used, for example, in drop-leaf tables.

Back saw or tenon saw
A saw used for small work on the bench-top.

Banding
Thin strips of different-coloured timbers made up in patterns and inlaid as a decorative feature into grooves cut in cabinetwork.

Bead
A semi-circular cut in a moulding.

Beadings
see mouldings

Beading saw
see gent's back saw

Beech
A light, reddish-brown wood with straight, fine, close grain. Beech is fairly hard, and is very popular for tools and furniture in general.

Blind-stitching
A technique of stitching used around the edges of stuffed furniture.

Blitz saw
A small saw with a thin blade designed for cutting metal, but also used for wood and plastics. It has a small hook at the end so that both hands can be used to operate it.

Block plane
A small plane used on end grain.

Bow saw
A narrow saw set in a wooden frame, used for cutting curves.

Boxwood
A hard, close-grained wood, ideal for chisel handles.

Braid
An ornamental strip of fabric, such as woven silk or wool, used as decoration along the edges of upholstered items.

Brocatelle
A heavy brocade whose design is in deep relief.

Bull-nose plane
A plane for cutting close into a corner. The cutter is very near to the front of the plane.

Burnisher
A hard, steel rod used to turn over the burr on scraping tools.

Burl or burr
An excrescence found on many trees, usually formed around an injury to the trunk. It is valued for use in veneers.

Butt chisel
A short-bladed chisel used when cutting housings for butt hinges.

Butt gauge
A device for marking out when hinging.

Butt hinge
A hinge with two matching leaves, each recessed into one of the pieces of wood to be joined – for example, a desk lid and the main body of the desk. When the lid is closed, the two leaves of the hinge are flat up against each other.

Butt joint
A joint in which two pieces of wood are joined lengthwise without overlap or tongue.

Cabinet-scraper
A tool used to finish wood in preparation for painting or varnishing.

Carcase
The skeleton of a piece of cabinetwork.

C-clamp
see G-clamp

Chamfering
Cutting a square edge equally on both sides of a piece of wood so as to form a bevel.

Circular plane
see compass plane

Clamp or cramp
A tool which holds pieces of wood or other items together.

Combination plane
see multi-plane

Compass plane
Sometimes called a circular plane, this has a flexible sole which can be set for convex or concave cutting.

Compass saw
A thin, taper-bladed saw used for cutting tiny holes.

Contact adhesives
Everyday adhesives used mainly for making quick and lasting repairs to plastics.

Cramp
see clamp

Cross-cut
A saw used for cutting across the grain of wood.

Curl
Feather grain found in various woods, most notably in mahogany.

Damask
A reversible fabric woven with patterns.

Deal
A word used loosely to describe wood cut from pine or fir logs.

Diffuse-reflection glass
A type of glass whose surface contains countless microscopic pits so that it fails to reflect a glare when brightly lit. This type of glass is much used in picture-framing.

Dovetail joint
A joint formed by one or more tapering projections (dovetails) on one board, fitted tightly into mortises carved into another.

Dowel
A round pin or peg used in jointing.

Dralon velvet
Imitation velvet made from Dralon, trade name for a fabric made from a mixture of cotton and synthetic fibres. Dralon velvet has the advantage that, unlike traditional velvet, it can be washed.

Drop-in seat
In a chair, a seat that has been constructed as a separate entity from the rest of the chair. Sometimes drop-in seats have been tacked in place, but often they can be simply removed by knocking them out.

Dual stone
An oilstone, having a rough texture on one side and a fine texture on the other.

English webbing
Webbing made from strips of fabric – unlike Pirelli webbing, which is made from strips of rubber.

Epoxy adhesives
Adhesives based on an epoxy (or epoxide) resin or several such resins. They are of limited use in cabinetmaking, but can come in useful for quick repairs.

Fadding
Laying on the first layer of French polish. Traditionally this is done with a burnisher, but most people find it easier to brush the French polish on.

Fillet
A strip of wood added to the work as either a guide or a support.

Float glass
A type of glass made by floating molten glass on a liquid of higher density so that it hardens into a flat sheet.

Fluteroni
A wide, U-shaped, carving gouge with round corners, used for shaping round sides.

Fore plane
A plane of length between those of the jack plane and the trying plane.

Frame saw
A saw with a narrow blade tensioned and supported in a wooden frame.

French polish
A solution of shellac in alcohol used to give furniture a shiny finish. The alcohol evaporates to leave a thin coating of shellac on the piece.

Fretsaw
A small saw that looks rather like a miniature hacksaw. It can be useful for cutting ornamental work or, in certain circumstances, for cutting holes in sheets of wood.

Furnishing fabric
A catch-all name covering chintzes, plain or patterned, heavy-duty fabrics and various manmade fabrics.

Garnet paper
One of the coarsest types of abrasive papers.

G-clamp or C-clamp
Used for small clamping work, these clamps get their names because of their shapes.

Gent's back saw
A small saw with a round handle and a thin blade, used for cutting dovetails and for other small work.

Gesso
A pigmented plaster which can be formed into a moulding, as in a picture frame.

Gooseneck scraper
Named for its general appearance, this is a scraper that is invaluable for cleaning certain types of mouldings and other shaped pieces of wood.

Grit size
A measure of the roughness of an abrasive paper. The lower the figure given for the grit size the coarser the paper.

Hacksaw
A saw used for cutting metals and plastics.

It has a thin, steel blade held in a U-shaped frame to which a handle is attached.

Hardwood
Wood from a deciduous tree.

Heartwood
The best timber. It comes from the heart of the tree and has matured with age.

Hessian
A plain-woven, coarse fabric made from jute or hemp.

Hickory
A whitish-yellow wood which is very tough, hard, elastic and strong. It is widely used for the handles of hammers.

Hogging
The rough planing of timber, usually using a jack plane that has a slightly rounded cutter.

Honing guide
see sharpening guide

Inlay
A form of decoration where pieces of wood and other materials are set into a base of wood and rendered flush.

Jack plane
The most commonly used plane. It gets its name from the expression 'Jack of all trades'.

Jigsaw
A saw with a thin, steel blade which is used for cutting intricate curves.

Jointer
A long plane that is particularly useful when planing long boards.

Keying
An addition to a piece of wood, used to strengthen it. Dovetail keying is where the piece of wood is inserted into a dovetailed housing to prevent a board from warping.

Keyhole saw
A saw similar to the compass saw, having a thin, tapering blade. It is used for cutting keyholes and similar slots.

Leaded lights
Panes of glass held together with lead strips of an H-shaped cross-section. Leaded lights are frequently found in the windows of old houses or on the fronts of antique dressers.

Lengthening bar
An addition used with a sash clamp to give added capacity.

Log saw
A thin-bladed saw with a tubular frame used for logging and large, rough work.

Macaroni
A wide, U-shaped, carving gouge with square corners, designed for finishing the sides of shallow recesses.

Mahogany
A fairly hard, reddish-brown timber of many varieties. Mahogany is used both for furniture and as a base for veneering.

Marbling
Using paint or ink to create the appearance or general effect of variegated marble.

Marquetry
A pattern made of inlaid veneers of wood, ivory, metal or other substance in order to form a picture or design. The word 'marquetry' refers also to the art of making such pictures or designs.

MDF (Mass-density fibreboard)
A manmade board used in mainly in making kitchen and bathroom cabinets. It has limited uses in furniture restoration.

Mitre
A joint formed by cutting the edges of two pieces of timber at an equal angle – usually 45°.

Mitre square
A tool used to test and mark lines at an angle of 45°.

Mortise
A usually rectangular slot or recess cut into a piece of timber and designed to receive a male part, or tenon.

Mortise chisel or registered pattern
A strong chisel specially designed for

cutting mortises. It has a thicker blade than the standard, plus a steel hoop and ferrule to hold the blade securely in the handle and protect the handle from splitting.

Mouldings or beadings
Pieces of timber with a preshaped profile, used for the edgings of furniture.

Multi-plane or combination plane
A plane capable of ploughing, rebating, beading and tonguing.

Oilstone
A fine-grained stone, lubricated with oil, which is used for sharpening cutting edges.

Oilstone slip
A shaped oilstone which is used for sharpening gouges.

Overstuffing
A technique frequently used in the construction of upholstered chairs. The springs are attached to the webbing, covered with fibre and held down by a coarse covering; then a further layer of stuffing is added before the final hessian covering.

Palm plane
A small plane which fits comfortably into the hand. It is useful when dealing with smaller, intricate work.

Parquetry
A geometric pattern constructed from inlaid pieces of wood, often of different textures and colours.Parquetry is most frequently employed in flooring.

Pearls
The granules in which animal glue is sometimes supplied.

Piano hinge
Essentially a butt hinge, but with leaves that are considerably longer.

Pirelli webbing
Webbing made from strips of rubber rather than from fabric.

Plinth
The receding part of a cabinet next to the floor.

Plough
A plane for making grooves or rebates.

PVC (or white woodworker's adhesive)
A frequently used adhesive which has as its base a synthetic resin called polyvinyl acetate.

Quick gouge
A deep-carving gouge for roughing-out.

Quilted tapestry
Tapestry woven in two layers to give a heavy, embossed appearance.

Rabbet
see rebate

Rail
The horizontal member of a frame.

Rebate or rabbet
A cut made on the edge of a frame or board to receive a sheet of glass or a wooden panel.

Rebate plane
A plane which can be fitted with different blades, used to cut grooves and rebates in high-quality furniture.

Registered pattern
see mortise chisel

Rip saw
A saw with special teeth designed for use when cutting with the grain.

Rosewood
A beautiful, dark, purplish-brown-coloured wood used for expensive cabinetwork, tool handles and other components.

Router
A hand or machine tool used to make a variety of cuts.

Sash clamp
Large clamp used to hold major components of furniture.

Sawhorse
A stand used to hold wood while it is being sawed. It is now possible to buy manufactured sawhorses which also feature

vices and other ancillary gadgets.

Saw set
A pincer-like tool that is used for setting saw teeth.

Scraper plane
A device rather like a spokeshave, but used to remove varnish and paint rather than wood.

Scratchstock
A small too! used to cut shallow recesses for inlaying.

Scrim
Open-weave cotton or linen fabric used for curtains, drapes etc.

Set
The inclination of alternate teeth of a saw from left to right. The term is used also for the distance that the cap iron is set back from the cutting edge of a plane.

Sharpening guide (or honing guide)
A device used when sharpening the blades of chisels or planes. It holds the blade against the oilstone at the correct angle.

Sheet glass
A type of glass made in cylindrical form and then flattened out. It is of interest to the furniture-maker because it has flaws and therefore character.

Shoulder plane
A precision plane which cuts across the grain to trim end grain before jointing.

Silicon-carbide paper
see wet-and-dry paper

Skew chisel
A chisel used for planing wood between lathe centres, squaring, beading, curving and tapering.

Slow gouge
A shallow-carving gouge for finishing work.

Softwood
Wood from a coniferous tree.

Spokeshave
A cutting tool with two handles, used for small, curved work. Its effect is similar to that of a plane.

Strings
Tiny strips of thin wood, square or rectangular in cross-section, used in inlaying.

Synthetic-resin adhesives
Adhesives based on synthetic resins which are supplied in two parts - a thick, syrupy liquid and a hardener.

Tapestry
A heavy, ornamental fabric.

Tenon
The male part of a mortise joint.

Toothing
The roughing-up of the surface of wood in order to provide keying for veneers.

Trying plane
A long, bench plane used in the same way and for the same purposes as a jointer.

Tungsten-carbide grit
The ultimate in manmade, abrasive grits, used for abrasive papers and wheels.

Tweed
A coarse, wool fabric, woven usually in two or more colours.

Uraldehyde glues
A type of slow-setting adhesive that is very useful in furniture repairing.

Valance
A short curtain of drapery hung along a piece of furniture both for decoration and to hide structural detail.

Velcro
Trade name for a type of fastening made of two nylon strips. One has a coarse surface, whereas the other is made up of countless tiny hooks, so that when the two surfaces are pushed together they form a bond which is strong but can nevertheless easily be ripped open whenever desired.

Veneer
Thin piece of wood glued to a solid timber background for the purposes of decoration. This allows you to use rare and exotic woods which either are not available in solid form or would be too expensive.

Veneering hammer
A tool used when gluing veneers to flatten them down and assist the joining.

Veneer punch
A punch used in making repairs to veneers.

Veiner
A tiny, deep, U-shaped gouge used in texturing and veining.

Vice (or vise)
A device, usually featuring a pair of jaws, designed to hold wood or other material while work is being done on it.

Warping
The twisting of timber as it dries.

Wax polish
A polish, used on furniture, which contains various synthetic waxes, as well as, if of highest-quality, natural beeswax.

Webbing
Strong, fabric strips of hemp, cotton, jute or rubber used as a support under springs.

Wet-and-dry paper
A type of abrasive paper that can be used wet. The grit is silicon carbide, and the paper and glue are waterproof.

White woodworker's adhesive
see PVA

INDEX

ACKNOWLEDGMENTS

DEMONSTRATION CREDITS
Leslie Charteris
Malcolm Hopkins
Leslie Howes
Sarah Nagy
Mark Treasure

EQUIPMENT CREDITS
Draper tools Ltd.,Black & Decker,
Buck and Ryan, J D Beardmore, Mr Price.
S Tysacks, Bellenger and Price Ltd.

Special thanks to Bob Cocker, Jan Orchard
and Paul Forrester.

PICTURE CREDITS
Page 11, top right: M Dunne, Elizabeth
Whiting and Associates; page 65, bottom left:
Tim Street Porter, Elizabeth Whiting and
Associates; page 91, bottom right: Maddox;
pages 105 and 112, cane and *papier-mâché*
chairs: Karin Craddock; page 180, top left:
M Dunne, Elizabeth Whiting and Associates.

While every effort has been made to ensure
that the information in this book is correct at
the time of going to press, the publisher cannot
accept responsibility for any inaccuracies.